THE BOOK OF
FLOWER ARRANGING

THE BOOK OF FLOWER ARRANGING

FRESH, DRIED, AND ARTIFICIAL

MARY FORSELL

COURAGE
BOOKS
AN IMPRINT OF
RUNNING PRESS
PHILADELPHIA, PENNSYLVANIA

A Friedman Group/Courage Book

Copyright © 1987, 1988 by Michael Friedman Publishing Group, Inc.

9 8 7 6 5 4 3 2

Digit on the right indicates number of this printing

ISBN 0-89471-678-6

THE BOOK OF FLOWER ARRANGING: FRESH, DRIED, AND ARTIFICIAL
was prepared and produced by
Michael Friedman Publishing Group, Inc.
15 West 26th Street
New York, New York 10010

Art Director/Designer: Mary Moriarty
Production Manager: Karen L. Greenberg
Photography: Bo Parker, John Deane, and Tony Cenicola
Everlasting Arrangements by Diana Penzner
Fresh Arrangements by Surroundings
Artificial Arrangements by un Jardin…en Plus

Color separations by Hong Kong Scanner Craft Company, Ltd.
Printed and bound in Hong Kong by Leefung Asco Printers, Ltd.

This book may be ordered from the publisher
Please include $1.50 postage
(But try your bookstore first.)

Published by Courage Books, an imprint of
Running Press Book Publishers
125 South Twenty-Second Street,
Philadelphia, Pennsylvania 19103.

ISBN 0-89471-678-6

DEDICATION

To Arthur, Burke, and Earl,
whose floral expertise was inspirational

CONTENTS

BO PARKER

BO PARKER

There are many schools of flower arranging—traditional, ikebana, contemporary—and their varieties attest to the endless combinations in which flowers can be arranged. For anyone who has ever found it confusing to sift through the vast quantities of information on the subject, or has been unable to choose one flower design volume because of the wide variety of books that address arranging, here is a unique book concept. *The Book of Flower Arranging* is the first volume to emphasize the many types of flower arranging materials that are available today—fresh, dried, and artificial flowers as well as such accessories as foliage, fruits, and vegetables—and to present designs that equally incorporate all of these materials. Unlike books that focus on fresh, dried, or artificial flowers, this volume recognizes that all have equal merits and uses in floral design. No book could be a full compendium of design ideas for every possible school or medium of design, but this volume takes a representative sampling from a variety of visual perspectives and offers clear direction on the use and integration of various design elements. Recognizing that floral design has reached new realms of experimentation, it takes the arranger on a step-by-step journey through the many design possibilities.

Of course, designing with the many intriguing forms of flowers involves a certain knowledge of the mechanics and processes of flower design, and the book recognizes this aspect too. It begins by offering an overview of design concepts and principles, such as rhythm, line, and harmony, explaining how these and other factors function within a design. This volume also addresses the various schools of flower design and shows how each can offer a wealth of design ideas to the arranger. Discussions of color and how a container relates to a design are followed by solid advice on how to work with fresh, dried, and artificial flowers.

Then, nine elegant and varied step-by-step arrangements are presented in rich color photographs that reveal the secrets behind the floral designer's work. And a final chapter brings it all together, showing how fresh, dried, and artificial flowers belong together in arrangements. Here a number of exciting ideas for combining these three types of flowers are included.

Intended both for the novice designer who wants to take a wide-ranging sampling of many types of flower arranging as well as for the experienced designer who wants a condensed and easily accessible source of design ideas, this volume is a wide-ranging examination of flower design, condensed into easy-to-follow directions and arrangements. It intends to teach and to inspire, but in no way to limit the arranger.

Left: A careful blending of materials of harmonious colors and the use of a striking yet simply designed container give this arrangement its charm. Roses provide a classic touch while waxflowers and brodiaea lend the bouquet a casual air. *Above:* The grouping of analogously colored arrangements subtly heightens the characteristic texture of each flower. The identical vase unites the three designs.

9

BASIC PRINCIPLES OF ARRANGING

JOHN DEANE

Before you begin arranging, you must be aware of the importance of key elements and principles of floral design. Similar to the principles of any kind of designing—whether it's interior design, fashion, painting and photographic composition, or even garden design—these basic ideas can guide the arranger to combining flowers and determining their various placements within a container. Although flowers grow in random abundance in nature, when isolated in individual designs, they take on a new aspect and require special treatment. Attention must be paid to the integration of forms, lines, and colors. Any arrangement, therefore, no matter how seemingly simplistic, embodies many design elements.

Despite all the rules to learn and techniques to master, however, floral design is primarily an intuitive and personal art. By practice, repetition, and experimentation, you'll come to sense when you've arranged every component to perfection.

ELEMENTS OF ARRANGING

The five elements of floral design are form, space, line, texture, and color. They are intrinsic to every arrangement, and an understanding of how they influence each other is essential to "good" design. In many designs, some elements may override others in importance. Even though these basic components of a design seem to blend together, upon more in-depth examination of an arrangement it becomes clear that each element makes a distinct contribution.

Form refers to the shape of the design and describes not only the width and height, but also the depth. These factors are part of the overall three-dimensional geometry of a design, which can range from the straightforward line to curves and circles, and to triangular shapes that include cones and pyramids.

A line form is often used in corsages and is also a basic aspect of distinctly upright designs. Such designs are usually accentuated by a slim, straight vase that won't detract from the beauty of the flowers.

Curves are found in S-shaped arrangements, where the arranging material curves subtly in opposite directions. Crescents are also forms of curves.

Circles are widely used in formal, continental-style designs, where all elements radiate from a recognizable center. Variations on the circle include oblong shapes and half circles.

Triangular and conical shapes lend dramatic impact to arrangements. Triangles can be either symmetrical or asymmetrical. Sometimes, a larger triangle is used in combination with another smaller one on the base to form a diamond shape. A conical shape is rounded on the bottom.

All of these shapes can be combined with others in a design. Lines can intersect triangles or radiate from circles; curves can sweep through conical shapes—the possibilities are limitless.

The forms of individual flowers can heighten the overall form of a design. Round forms—such as phlox, marigolds, and daisies—lend themselves well to circular and curve-filled de-

Left: In this artificial design of chrysanthemums, agapanthus, and thistle, a complementary color scheme is used. Pastel yellow chrysanthemums are soothingly juxtaposed with purple agapanthus. Dark purple agapanthus are placed in the middle of the arrangement, and lavender filler blooms reach upward around the sides. The orange-red thistle allow the yellow aspect of the complementary scheme to dominate. Above: A variety of forms contributes to the look of this traditional wildflower design. Focal star-shaped lilies, yellow button-shaped tansy flowers, purple ageratum, and a mixture of filler flowers all come together in a continuous rhythmic flow. The cattails enliven the design by extending beyond the basic circular form and echoing the rich, rusty color of the terra-cotta container.

signs. Spike flowers—such as snapdragons, gladiolus, delphiniums, liatris, and stock—provide dramatic lines and angles in a design. When rounded and spiked forms are used together, however, remember to place round flowers below spiked flowers for a more balanced effect.

The second design element, *space*, at first seems like a simplistic concept. But, as experts will attest, the void left between each flower, green, or branch is as necessary as are the materials themselves. Even in arrangements that incorporate a profusion of design elements, space plays a vital role, however subtly. Space is used to draw attention to the individual loveliness of different elements and groupings within an arrangement. A spare arrangement places a great deal of emphasis on space, while one that is too crowded can actually diminish the visual effectiveness of the individual elements.

Line, too, is vital in a design as it outlines an arrangement. The difference between line and form is that form describes shapes within the boundaries while line traces the boundaries of a design. Lines can be curved, triangular, or simply an assemblage of straight, vertical lines; they can accent color and lend dramatic impact to an arrangement. For example, lines of purple liatris cutting across and extending beyond a mass of round yellow mums not only creates a strong color contrast but also produces an unusual outline that actually heightens the roundness of the mums and the spikiness of the liatris. To draw attention to a particular area of a design, many materials can be used: manzanita wood, branches of all kinds, pussy willow, curly willow—which combine lines with curves—all spike flowers, and all flowers with long, dramatic stems. Dried arrangements, in particular, place a strong emphasis on line because they often incorporate long, twisted branches and greens such as eucalyptus, liatris, delphinium, and willow.

BO PARKER

Left: In this ikebana-derived design, the sharp upward movement of the pink nerine lilies and allium is balanced by the freely flowing arches created by the grass. The low bowl is a very unobtrusive element in the arrangement and creates the appearance of flowers growing naturally. The camouflaging base of cymbidium orchids and fresh green leaves further suggests "nature's way."

Below: Dried flowers are especially conducive to creating arrangements that hold their shape. Here, delphinium contributes expressive linear forms while the greenery subtly interweaves between the flowers, creating a pleasing balance to the lavender and pink. A design such as this one can provide year-round beauty in a home or office setting.

TONY CENICOLA

Dried arrangements also strongly emphasize *texture*, the fourth element of floral design. Texture refers to the smoothness or complexity of the surface of a design material. For example, satiny smooth silk tulips have a completely different tactile quality than thistle. The texture of an arranging material is as important as its shape when determining what other flowers it is best combined with and how it should be displayed. An elegant tropical orchid is much more regally displayed in a cut-crystal vase than in a basket; a wildflower, on the other hand, is at home in a fiber basket, a cream pitcher, or even in a homespun, makeshift container.

Textures within a design can sometimes be heightened by the juxtaposition of varied surfaces. For example, an artificial silk flower combined with twisted and furrowed dried flowers produces a texture-rich design when the elements are carefully selected.

Color is perhaps the most obvious and most appreciated element of an arrangement. Nature provides such an endless and startling array of colors that the arranger can never possibly feel limited by the same old combinations. New hybrid flowers are constantly being developed to add an even greater array of shades to fresh flowers. Artificial flowers boast everlasting colors that can be added to any fresh-flower design to give it new life. And dried flowers, too, possess a wide yet subtle selection of colors. As flowers dry, their colors will either fade or alter slightly. These changes can result in some very interesting shades of the original colors. Purple flowers will often dry to a black color that can be further dramatized with the addition of glossy lacquer or watercolor streaks of red or yellow; some dried flowers arrive on the market bleached to a stunning white shade that would be impossible to achieve and maintain in nature; and dried leaves that are treated with glycerine take on beautiful quartz-like striations that are of far greater interest than are the original colors.

Color will determine the success or failure of a design because it is so vivid an element. The old decorating rule of thumb holds true for flower designs as well: complementary colors, which are generally defined as cool (blues and greens) and warm (reds and oranges), work best together. There are many colors that fall in between and many other aspects of color to consider, however, and these will be further discussed in Chapter 2.

This fresh arrangement plays on a variety of textures: the smoothness of the lilies, freesia, and alstroemeria; the furled complexity of the rambling roses; the intricate surfaces of the Queen Anne's lace; and the rough, cactuslike qualities of the spiky club moss. However, the design is balanced by an emphasis on the focal flowers and by the use of filler flowers to tie the many textures together.

*Above: Dried hydrangea are a daringly different design element that should be used in a bold manner. Here, the autumnal colors of the flowers are highlighted by like-colored eucalyptus berries and foliage. The large scale of the flowers calls for an oversized vase, which is neutrally colored so as not to upstage the subtle coloration of the arrangement. **Right:** Many elements and principles of design are at work in this lively artificial composition. The slightly asymmetrical form is in harmony with the surprising liveliness of the complementary color scheme in which orange and yellow daffodils, crocuses, primulas, and daisies dominate, and pinkish lavender crocuses provide stunning contrast. The casual arrangement is effectively displayed in a simple basket, which helps unify the design. The principle of rhythm is also apparent here, with the eye moving easily around the arrangement from the daisies and primulas, which form the foundation, to the blooming daffodils and crocuses.*

PRINCIPLES OF ARRANGING

Rather than being fundamental parts of a design, principles are qualities that the arranger brings to a design, adding the finishing touches to the basic elements, manipulating nature to create a new level of perfection. The principles are balance, unity, scale, accent, harmony, and rhythm.

To achieve *balance* in a design, the arranger must consider several aspects of the whole. An arranger must complement a design's container in terms of height and general characteristics of flowers. For example, balance may be achieved by creating a central line in a design and surrounding it with materials in mirror-image symmetry. An arranger should also consider coloration and shape of design materials and how these elements create balance. For example, darker flowers seem more weighty and are best placed at the bottom or center of an arrangement; lighter-colored flowers are good choices for strong vertical elements, which push upward and outward from a design to create a greater sense of height.

Balance is also an important consideration from a practical standpoint. Flowers, greens, branches, and other materials should be appropriately placed in a container so that there is no chance that the design will topple. Stability can be given to a design by clear or colored marbles, bags of sand, or foam.

Unity is created when all aspects of the design are successfully integrated. This is a particularly challenging yet pleasurable aspect of combining fresh, artificial, and dried flowers because the various textures, colors, and general visual distinctions between the flowers, branches, and greens of the three media can make choosing a container and juxtaposing the materials very tricky. However, the advantage of having artificial flowers and everlastings on hand is that these materials retain their beauty and therefore can be used on the spur of the moment to help unify fresh flower designs.

Designs incorporating such everyday flowers as cornflowers, marigolds, and petunias can be unified by the addition of a rustic-looking burlap ribbon, pods, and pine cones, or an

unpretentious container, such as a basket or simple bowl. Designs that include such delicate-looking flowers as roses, orchids, or calla lilies call for simple, elegant glass containers and such exquisite filler flowers as Queen Anne's lace, statice, and high-quality ribbon.

Scale, the third principle of floral design, is the harmonious, proportional grouping of all parts of the design. Large flowers within the design must not completely overshadow smaller ones. This is not to say that small flowers cannot be used with large ones: Small flowers can be massed to create a more powerful presence while still retaining their delicacy.

Another aspect of scale is the proportionate relationship of the flower to the vase. A long-stemmed lily should not tower unsteadily in a bud vase; similarly, a small agapanthus is completely dwarfed by a tall container. A good example of the perfect scale relationship is the miniature arrangement: Small as these designs are—sometimes no taller than three inches— they follow all of the basic elements and principles of design and generally use bud vases for a few small-size blooms.

A third aspect of scale is how a design relates to its surroundings. A design that includes "high-construction" techniques—that is, the use of a multitude of flowers in an oversized container—is usually best displayed in a wide-open space with high ceilings such as a restaurant or lobby. By contrast, miniature arrangements should be placed where they do not have to compete with a clutter of objects. Placing a miniature on a small shelf or tray against a neutral background retains the visual impact of the arrangement.

Harmony is another essential principle of floral design. It describes the way materials of an arrangement work together. While unity defines how different materials blend together, harmony deals with how different materials are contrasted and joined together in a composition. Harmony not only stresses the use of similar shapes, but also requires variation of elements so that the differences between materials are further heightened and can be appreciated. Spiky flowers such as liatris and tuberose can provide an overpowering linear arrangement if not harmonized with round shapes like scabiosas and peonies. Similarly, a monochromatic design of yellow carries more impact with the addition of orange, red, and pink, which are complementary colors. Strong use of pastel colors also creates a harmonious design.

Rhythm is accomplished when the eye is drawn gently and pleasingly throughout the floral composition. The viewer reacts to a thoughtfully composed design by naturally sensing the transitions between elements. Rhythm draws the eye from bolder to subtler elements.

The final principle of floral design, *accent,* is created by the use of a flower or grouping of flowers that is dominant in color, size, or shape. Such a flower or grouping encompasses the focal point, or visual focus, of a design. A single, large iris or lily placed among less dominant flowers becomes the accent of a design. However, with flowers of equal size, the one with the dominant color will create the accent.

Although rhythm, harmony, and unity are vital ingredients in an arrangement, they need a dominant force to hold them together and give the eye a resting place. Accent breaks the monochromatic and monospatial tendencies of some designs, creating a core or central place in an arrangement.

The individual loveliness of each flower in this design is heightened by the use of contrasting forms. The color scheme, however, also brings together all of the elements to create a visual harmony. The varied forms of the lilies, scabiosas, tulips, delphinium, and freesia are united through their pastel colors. Additionally, the Queen Anne's lace and caspia help tie the design together. Ivy provides contrast while harmonizing with the foliage of the flowers.

JOHN DEANE

Above: The rhythmic associations of naturally growing camellias are captured in this artificial design. Without the encumbrance of a variety of flowers to view, the eye is easily drawn around the arrangement, savoring not only the individual beauty of each camellia bloom, but also the wonderful juxtapositions of flower, foliage, and bud. The elegance of the silver container emphasizes the regal posturing of the flowers.

Right: One very effective way of creating a focal point is by using a brightly colored, oversized bloom. An impressive red lotus dominates this Oriental design. Graceful white orchids provide asymmetric contrast, and charming round foliage heightens the effect of the globular container.

THE FOCAL POINT

The focal point is the part of the design that results when the principle of accent is applied. Establishing a primary focus of an arrangement can be achieved through a variety of methods, usually through manipulating colors or shapes.

A focal point can consist of a number of flowers grouped together to form an eye-catching center. For example, grouping lilies of different colors, with centers facing outward, will immediately grab the viewer's attention because of the contrast of colors among the striking forms. Additionally, using ordinary circular forms that boast bright colors, such as zinnias and carnations, will command focal-point attention. Unusual flowers like heliconia, anthurium, or calla lilies can also command attention as both their forms and colors are strong elements.

A focal point can be emphasized by the building up of striking forms around it. Asymmetrical triangles flanking a flower or group of flowers will successfully direct attention to the focal point between them. The juncture of any two distinct shapes or the cutting of an element through an open space can also create a focal point.

Some flowers are meant to be focal points. Single-blossomed flowers—roses, peonies, gardenias, lilies, and others—draw attention because of their striking forms, colors, shapes, and sizes. They can create an effective point of visual juncture in groupings as well. A solitary open rose surrounded by three lilies is a stunning arrangement. To heighten the effect, try surrounding focal flowers with half-opened flowers (tulips and roses are particularly effective) radiating in strong lines from the center. When selecting focal flowers, try to choose those with the darkest colors and the heaviest heads to ensure that they effectively command focal attention without clashing with the other flowers.

The symmetric, triangular design is a mainstay of traditional flower arranging. Wildflowers define the outer areas of this design along with pink liatris spikes, which elegantly point outward, emphasizing the triangular form. Elegantine, cosmos, and freesia are blended in a pastel scheme of pink, lavender, and yellow. Because they are artificial flowers, it is easy to position them in a symmetrical framework. The long-necked, pastel pink ceramic container suggests an inverted, mirror-image of the flowers above.

ARRANGEMENT STYLES

Just as interiors have moods created by the arrangement of furniture and objects as well as by color schemes, flowers can be arranged in many different styles with numerous variations on each. Many floral styles have developed in the long and fascinating history of flower design. It is not possible to allot each one a separate category and discuss each in depth because each style carries with it a very detailed history and list of principles. Therefore, this book will simply refer to three wide-ranging categories for discussion: traditional, encompassing styles from many cultures; ikebana; and contemporary.

These descriptions are intended as inspirational starting points from which you can improvise.

Traditional

Traditional refers to the many Western styles of the past that encourage symmetry of design as well as lavish use of a variety of flowers and colors. Also referred to as Continental or Formal, such designs may feature smoothly curved round forms or perfectly proportioned triangles that emphasize balance and harmony. Primarily inspired by French designs, traditional forms were in vogue in both Europe and North America from the seventeenth to the nineteenth centuries. Because they are truly classics, however, such designs are still effective today and are constantly being updated.

Certain classic flowers such as roses, lilies, and orchids were generally used in the past in traditional designs. However, flowers of all types, especially focal flowers (see previous page) that command attention are effective elements in traditional designs. Aside from focal points, wild flowers—if used effectively and in a sophisticated manner—can be included in traditional designs.

Two types of color schemes were favored in the past: bold, royal colors—encompassing everything from ruby red to deep purple—and pastel blues, pinks, yellows, and greens, with white added. As long as the scheme is carried out in symmetrical form, however, a wide range of colors can be used today.

Containers, too, play an important role in determining the effectiveness of a traditional design. A regal silver bowl, especially if it is footed, will elevate a design to give it a timeless, traditional look. Also, containers with bubble-like bottoms topped by long necks will imbue a design with a touch of formal prominence. Other appropriate containers include anything that has symmetrical proportions and is made of classic, finished materials. Cut crystal, silver, and finely glazed porcelain are good choices; epergnes, footed bowls, and urn shapes also carry traditional associations.

An extension of traditional design was practiced by the nineteenth-century Edwardians. The floral arrangers of this time favored two-tiered arrangements. In this style, fruits and vegetables act as a base and are topped by a central candlestick surrounded by blooms and foliage that radiate upwards. Ornate silver-plated stands with flat, circular tops act as containers.

Another equally complex offshoot of traditional design was inspired by the paintings of the Flemish school of the seventeenth century. Rich colors, elaborate mixtures of flowers and foliage, and ornate footed containers characterize this very sophisticated school of design.

JOHN DEANE

In the innovative field of flower design, styles are freely mixed to achieve stunning results. Here, roses, the most traditional of flowers, are grouped in a classic, balanced design. The surprise comes from the use of a glass container, which provides a modern twist to this very realistic artificial arrangement.

The crowning touch to traditional style's variations is the Victorian school. The Victorians, fond of profusion in every aspect, did not thoroughly embrace the symmetric designs, though the triangle was an important aspect of the arrangements of the day. They expanded on the traditional use of an abundance of materials by creating massive arrangements overflowing with flowers such as lilacs, roses, hyacinths and greens including ivy, rhododendron and eucalyptus leaves, and pink-tinged azalea foliage. Containers ranged from extremely detailed, oversized porcelains, bronzes, and Oriental pots to jardinieres and urns.

Aspects of all these styles are reemerging today as interior design places a greater emphasis on examining the styles of the past and creating "period" rooms. Such designs will add truly unique and eclectic touches around your home.

Ikebana

While ikebana is a very spare art that stresses simplicity, it is also highly formalized. This Japanese artform is one of the best examples of the importance of and stress on symbolism both in Japanese gardening and the broader Japanese culture.

The placement and spatial relationships between the elements play a very significant role in the design. These factors are meant to reflect the order of nature and the relative positions of earth, man, and heaven in the scheme of things. To effectively convey the symbolism, the use of flowers, foliage, branches, grasses, and mosses is extremely restrained. These materials are rarely found all together in an authentic ikebana design, although other designs can be successfully created based on the ikebana concept.

The floral components of ikebana designs are typically irises, Fuji mums, or lilies. Foliage, branches, and grasses accentuate the focal flowers by radiating upward and outward toward heaven. Natural accessories include stones and woods of all kinds—driftwood, curly willow, birch, etc.—as long as their forms express the symbolic role they play in the design. Many designs today are variations of ikebana that incorporate additional accessories such as shells, marbles, or whatever ornamental features seem appropriate without destroying the understated elegance and simplicity of the flowers in the designs. Although the conventional ikebana design generally includes just three of any one flower, you can use additional types and quantities of flowers in your designs without undermining their elegance.

Ikebana designs convey an exquisite fragility and beauty and also exemplify the principle of rhythm: The arrangement flows from flower to flower. Most ikebana designs have a basic triangular shape that lends itself to this rhythmic quality. Artificial flowers, in particular, are excellent choices for ikebana designs, because they can be so easily positioned in the gentle, expressive curves required in this art.

Top: A dramatic ikebana arrangement commands central attention in this very stark setting. The upward-reaching cattails, dried focal strawflower, flowering eucalyptus, and twisting bark interact serenely across the open spaces of the design. Bottom: Reminiscent of a still-life painting, this grouping of natural materials demonstrates contemporary design tenets. Today, designers freely use anything that occurs in nature as an object worthy of display. To create this vignette, a twig basket is filled with pine sprays, which flow dramatically over the side, highlighting the basket handle. Analogously colored objects—a woven mat and tray, sand-colored rocks, open clam shells, and wood—are grouped nearby. Right: Ikebana designs incorporate few elements but require great concentration in the positioning of materials. The use of a low, unobtrusive bowl emphasizes the importance of space and openness in a composition. This idea is further carried out by three graceful irises, which represent the relationship of man to heaven and earth. Subtly colored foliage echoes the positions of the flowers, while a snaking vine provides a note of stark complexity at the base of the design. The cluster of materials at the base is offset by the powerful effect of the upwardly pointing fruit branches. Note that artificial and dried materials are used very effectively in this design, which requires the precise placement of materials.

24

*Above: A vibrant miniature wooden vase from India and its contents—a few simple dried forms—demonstrate the principles of contemporary design. A vase can act as a focal point in a design, and flowers need not be dramatic, classic types to be effective. An arrangement of wildflowers and branches can have as much impact as that of traditional blooms. **Right:** Contemporary designs can take on many forms, but all are characterized by the free use of materials. In this bold composition, a variety of very strong forms are brought together. A full-flowered branch of cymbidium orchids reaches outward to the right of the design, while the other materials are free to go their own ways. Brilliant red firecracker and gloriosa lilies point in various directions while sumac establishes a base for the design. Star-of-Bethlehem flowers point decidedly upward, and their minimal, well-defined forms contrast effectively with the relative openness of the other flowers. Finally, the encircling grapevine provides a line of vision for the eye to glide along through this stunning design.*

Contemporary

The thought of contemporary arrangements conjures up a whole repertoire of images: bold, multiform designs of converging lines, circles, and triangles; sculptural, free-form compositions in which the unusual qualities of individual pieces are emphasized; and casual arrangements that allow space to be used freely. Contemporary designs almost defy description because every new design that innovatively uses flowers can be included among the contemporary range of styles. Contemporary designs usually provide an element of surprise and use materials in an inventive way, often combining elements from a number of different traditional styles.

This design style builds on the spare form of ikebana by taking unusual juxtapositions of flowers and echoing them throughout a design. Another ground-breaking aspect of contemporary design is the freedom to incorporate a wide range of accessories. Fruits and vegetables, grasses, woods, stones, vines, and shells are among the limitless array of materials that can be included. This free incorporation of unusual elements can sometimes also break established rules of de-

sign, for example, by juxtaposing very different kinds of elements such as very smooth flowers with twisted, pointed branches or using pastels alongside very primary colors.

Contemporary designs often use traditional flowers in striking new ways, such as adding a bouquet of fresh, loose lilies or gladiolus to a clear glass vase or bowl filled with marbles. This practice is known as *minimalism*, using one or two types of flowers in a simple yet striking way.

Artificial flowers are particularly liberating to use in contemporary designs because the flowers can be manipulated into bold, daring shapes. All "species" of artificial flowers are also available year round, so it is possible to create extremely unorthodox groupings of flowers.

Dried flowers, too, are often displayed to best advantage in contemporary designs. In dried arrangements, very modern-looking styles can be created with the use of large branches, fantastic pods, and other remarkable forms that are only possible in the dried state. Use of dried bamboo, wheats, and grasses alongside the rounded forms of protea and hydrangea will create a very contemporary sculptural effect.

COLOR

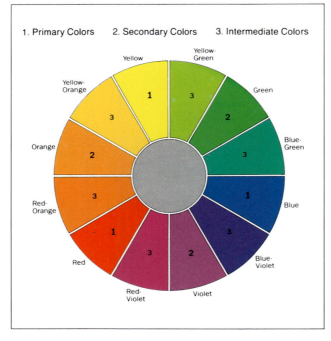

1. Primary Colors   2. Secondary Colors   3. Intermediate Colors

Color has a strong influence on everything people do. It is a basic aspect of people's perceptions, and each color carries with it certain emotions. Color indicates warmth and cold, signals directions, and generally draws or diverts attention. Because color is such a basic part of general perception, it is an extremely significant element of flower arranging. Arranging flowers helps you to increase color perception because you will be testing combinations as you design. Color conveys the tone of an arrangement. It can create cheerful or contemplative moods or make materials look delicate or dramatic; it can also emphasize lines and highlight textures. Because it is so influential in so many ways, color choice requires careful forethought. Using a color wheel is a good way to see how colors work together, whether they are primary, secondary, or intermediate.

PRIMARY COLORS

Flowers and foliage exhibit an amazing spectrum of colors with so many tints, shades, and tones that the idea of choosing correct color combinations may at first seem daunting to the amateur. The science of color, however, seems simpler to approach once you've realized that all colors are derived from red, blue, and yellow—the *primary colors*. They are equidistant from one another on the color wheel and form the basis for all other color combinations. Primary colors cannot be produced by combining other colors.

Red is a hot color and conveys strong emotions and qualities, whether they are passion, rage, or even healthfulness. It is used for festive occasions, such as Christmas or Valentine's Day or any occasion when the symbolism of the heart is appropriate.

Blue, a cool color, conjures images of sea and sky. It is therefore a timeless, elegant, and restful color. Paradoxically, blue can evoke feelings of serene happiness and optimism while it is also associated with sadness, but perhaps this is because of the other contemplative moods it evokes.

The third primary color, yellow, reflects a buoyant—even jubilant—mood. It bespeaks a certain innocence as well as evokes images of sunny warmth.

All together these three powerfully emotional colors make up the first triangle of the color wheel.

SECONDARY COLORS

Each primary color, mixed equally with the next, produces a *secondary color*. Red and yellow create orange; blue and red result in violet; and yellow and blue produce green.

Orange is less emotional than red and less forceful than yellow. This offspring of the two primary colors combines aspects of both. Orange does, however, have a very loud impact and looks best when tempered with such colors as gold, brown, red-orange, and other colors that suggest the feeling of autumn.

Violet is an often-used color. Like the colors that produce it, violet has a strong presence. But the pure vibrancy of blue and

Left: The color wheel demonstrates the gradations of hues that can be used in flower arrangements. *Above:* Color is the most influential element of flower designs. In this composition, materials of varying textures and forms are united by the use of a striking white color scheme. The pink on the stems of the dendrobium orchids and the green of the foliage is heightened by the white contrast. The subtle neutrality of the white flowers underscores the low-key sophistication of the overall design.

Left: Fiery red snapdragons, primulas, and ranunculus tinged with yellow and surrounded by rich green foliage exemplify how a variety of forms can be united with the use of common colors. Red and yellow, two primary colors, are brilliant elements in any design. The yellow also offsets the interplay of green and red, which are complementary colors. *Above:* This mass arrangement of flowers has a predominantly blue color scheme, making it a perfect summer design that will provide a soothing, cooling effect wherever it is placed. The analogously colored spike flowers provide an outward thrust, while the focal lily establishes the center of the arrangement. *Right:* The beautiful possibilities for monochromatic styling are displayed in the use of colors in this design. The fact that artificial flowers are not limited by season makes it possible to enliven an interior at any time of the year. Here, a vibrant yellow arrangement of tulips, chrysanthemums, primulas, and buttercups is complemented by a casual white wicker basket.

red is tempered to a lush mixture that can be contrasted with many colors in an arrangement.

Green is a lively color that directly conveys what it embodies in nature: life. Combining aspects of contemplative blue and buoyant yellow, green is an in-between color that has its own distinct personality. It is a prevalent color in designs because it is naturally at home with any color.

INTERMEDIATE COLORS

The six colors already described are known as the *spectrum hues*. Taken together, this group produces the *tertiary* or *intermediate colors*. They are named for their parents, with the appropriate primary color supplying the first name and the secondary color supplying the last name. These colors are blue-green, blue-violet, red-violet, red-orange, yellow-orange, and yellow-green.

Colors in themselves are referred to as *hues*. To further vary the twelve hues of the color wheel, white can be added to create a *tint*, or lightening, of a particular color. For instance, white and violet produce a lavender tint. Adding gray will produce a *tone*. When we tone something down, we reduce its intensity. Rose is a tone produced from red and gray. Introducing black will darken a color to produce a *shade*. Combining black and blue results in navy blue.

Below: Analogous orange, yellow, and green colors suggest the harvest of autumn and the vibrancy of nature in this artificial design. The way the lovely orange daisies spill over the sides of the charming basket further suggests the abundance of the harvest. The fruits demonstrate how natural accessories can be effortlessly united to a design if they have similar color, texture, or shape. **Right:** *Spiky line forms charge flower designs with energy by providing exciting upward movement. Here, similarly colored flowers in shades of purple and pink extend from a neutrally colored, elongated black vase, which unites perfectly with the flowers because of its strong shape.*

JOHN DEANE

Analogous color combinations are an effective means of evoking the seasons in floral designs. Here, charming artificial wildflowers and wheat in burgundy and muted orange pleasantly call to mind the brisk beauty of autumn.

Black, white, and gray are neutral colors and are often excellent choices as container colors. Black generally provides a forceful base for pale and bright colors and contributes a dramatic effect that does not actively draw attention to itself. A white container is the perfect choice for all-white arrangements or those with touches of white. Gray containers are effective for almost all designs, particularly when the tone of the dominant color harmonizes with the tone of the gray.

CHOOSING COLORS

There are several methods for choosing colors based on their relationships in the color wheel. Each combination implies different emotions by producing entirely different effects.

Monochromatic harmony encompasses a full range of one color. The hue is modified using white, gray, and black to produce tints, tones, and shades. For monochromatic designs,

the darkest color is generally used as a focal point, with the next darkest color surrounding it, and the lightest color on the outside. This color usage gives the arrangement a sense of unity and rhythm. In monochromatic designs, it is possible to use a variety of shapes and textures because unity is subtly reiterated by the harmonious, unstrained color scheme. The viewer's eye unites disparate shapes and textures through the rhythmic quality of the color. A fourth monochromatic color from the surrounding environment can also contribute to the overall harmony of a design. Monochromatic schemes are often the natural choice for dried arrangements because everlastings' colors are often variations of the same hue.

Another kind of color usage in arrangements is *complementary design*. Complementary colors are situated directly opposite one another on the color wheel. Such combinations are very familiar in the everyday environment, whether it is

34

This monochromatic design of purples has a very soothing effect on the eye. A vibrant massing of irises, dahlias, larkspur, lilacs, primulas, petunias, and sanguisorbas provides an imaginative variety of textures and forms. However, the effect of so many multivariegated forms is not overwhelming because the design is held together by the common color theme.

the classic red and green holiday combination, the dynamic pairing of orange and blue, or the often seen vibrancy of yellow and violet combinations. Such colors heighten each other's effects and provide very visually exciting and forceful harmonies. In fact, they visually complete one another because the secondary color in any complementary combination is composed of the two primary colors other than the one with which it is paired.

When arranging with these colors, remember that the synergism produced as a result of their combination does not mean that they should be equally paired in a design. Because they are directly opposite one another on the color wheel, these colors tend to lose their effectiveness if they are not unified by the dominance of one of them. There are many ways to vary the mix. If your choice of dominant color is violet, for example, you might try adding shades, tones, and tints of

violet to the design and then add just a few touches of orange. The use of a neutral container will further unify the effect. Artificial flowers are particularly wonderful to work with in such a situation. Just the right value of a color is needed to balance the design, and artificial flowers are available in a wide variety of color values. Because they never fade, these perfect, subtle color combinations are ensured for the life of the arrangement.

A third way of choosing colors is through the *triadic combination*. Triads consist of three hues that are located at equidistant points on the color wheel. These harmonies are composed of either all primary, secondary, or intermediate colors. Examples of triads are blue, red, and yellow, or orange, green, and violet. Because these combinations produce bold, uncompromising results, they should be combined with neutral fillers such as Queen Anne's lace, maidenhair, and statice

JOHN DEANE

Left: Subtle color contrasts are used in this open and rhythmic design of blue and violet forget-me-nots and delicate lunaria branches in a creamy, complementary color. The deepest color, a dark blue, is used for the container, while the focal color, a vibrant light blue, is employed in the center of the design. The lighter shades of violet and cream are appropriately used around the edges of the arrangement to lend it an airy quality.
Below: This compelling arrangement highlights the vibrancy of red, blue, and yellow. Numerous flowers—anemones, freesia, zinnias, and bachelor's-buttons—radiate outward from the focal point in a wheel of bright hues, unified by the neutral Queen Anne's lace and the black container.

BO PARKER

and a neutral container so that the resulting arrangement is not overwhelming. Another way of tempering these straightforward combinations is to vary their color values by using tints, tones, and shades to create a pleasingly unified effect.

Another very effective guideline for choosing color is the *analogous combination.* Analogous colors combine any three or four colors that are next to one another on the color wheel. Often seen in interior decorating, this use of color combinations is very popular because it allows for a wide range of colors and provides a rhythmic flow of associated hues. Analogous colors produce vignettes all their own. Red, orange, and yellow recall the fiery hues of autumn or the drama of a sunset. Purple, green, and blue are reminiscent of a nighttime scene in the forest. Because they have similar qualities, analogous colors are more easily unified by the eye than are complementary colors.

Keeping these basic principles in mind, you can go on to explore how colors are best matched in an arrangement to produce an overall effect. When choosing colors for arrangements, the first thing to consider is the balance of light and dark. A dozen red roses will overstimulate the eye if not unified by contrasts, such as green leaves. The red will remain the dominant color, but its effectiveness will be heightened by the addition of the leaves.

Another important rule of design is that the use of too many types and colors of flowers can create visual chaos. Colors and forms need to be repeated in a design to create rhythm. Also, if colors are equally combined—as can happen in complementary designs—the effect is a "striped" or divided composition. Therefore, one color should always dominate a composition. If three colors are used in a design, use more of the lighter and less of the darker color. An effective design using three colors would incorporate approximately 65 percent of the lightest color, 25 percent of the middle color, and 10 percent of the darkest, focal color. A liberal use of dark colors will result in a heavy, even somber-looking, design.

Also note that when darker colors are placed above light colors in a design, the light colors seem to be crushed under the weight of the darker colors. Therefore, colors should be distributed according to their visual effects, with darkest shades in the lower region of the design, attention-grabbing brighter shades acting as focal points slightly higher up in the design, and light colors acting as winglike devices, lifting the arrangement upward to create an airy effect.

A final aspect of color that should be stressed is the importance of matching arrangement colors with background colors. There are no definitive rules for choosing a background color. Generally, gray provides a unifying effect, while white tends to create too harsh an outline of an arrangement. A background color that extends one of the colors of the design is usually effective.

Although these basic guidelines will prove to be quite effective in determining color selection, do not be afraid to be daring in your choice of colors for a design. There is always something new to be learned in the interesting play of colors among different forms and textures.

The effect of this design is particularly enchanting because of the daring use of colors. A basic analogous scheme of yellow, orange, and green is enlivened by the bold usage of pink. Lavender thistle adds a cool element to the design. Such an enchanting color design virtually defies seasonal limitations. While the bright pink and yellow convey images of warmer weather—particularly that of spring and summer—the orange tones suggest the hues of autumn. However, this arrangement would also be appropriate in the depths of winter, with its colors foretelling the future flowering of spring.

BO PARKER

CONTAINERS

s an extension of the principles of unity, balance, and harmony, the choice of a container must be made with thoughtful attention paid to the mood of a design. A container should be chosen to complement a design. If it is not somehow related in color, texture, or shape to the arrangement, the artistic effect of the design will be lost.

Because a container should never overwhelm or underestimate the materials it holds, simple, unornamented designs are often the best choices. For formal designs, eye-catching containers that are integral to the elegance of the overall effect can be used. Generally, however, containers that are heavily decorated and vibrantly colored will eclipse a floral design.

The array of containers to choose from is indeed vast. Not only is there a multitude of shapes, but also, there are many choices of materials, including baskets, glass, ceramics, pottery, and metals. It would seem that so many choices could make selecting a repertoire of containers an in-depth project. However, as any seasoned flower arranger will attest, once you begin collecting containers, you develop a design sensibility that enables you to assemble a wide variety of usable styles.

The two most important factors in your selection of a container are size and aesthetic qualities. The first criterion is very practical. You should ensure that the container has a wide enough opening for the arrangement you envision. Also, consider the container's height in relation to your arranging materials, as it is essential that the two are in proportion if your design is to work. Traditionally speaking, the arrangement should be one-and-one-half times the height of the container, but this rule is not etched in stone.

Also consider the decorative appeal of the container. Its decoration should be in keeping with the style of the arrangement and should have a coloration that will unify the whole. If your arrangement is to consist of graceful, long-stemmed flowers, you would not want to choose a squat container; similarly, a basket is inappropriate for a Japanese ikebana flower arrangement, as these arrangements require low, open bowls. The same degree of formality or casualness as in the intended arrangement must be reflected in the container.

BASKETS

Among the many containers you can choose from today are baskets. Generally, the most inexpensive, and often the most effective and versatile of containers, baskets are available in a wide range of shapes, sizes, and fiber combinations. Additionally, the colors of baskets are easily altered with spray paint; they can also be lacquered for a more finished appearance. Unlike the neutral role that other containers usually play, baskets can act as an enlivening component of a design. A basket overflowing with an abundance of flowers whose focal color is red can be spray painted to match this dominant color.

Inherently charming, baskets often have unusual, variegated textures that reflect one-of-a-kind craftsmanship. This homespun aspect of baskets should be played up in a design that uses flowers with interesting and varied textures. Wild-

Left: White containers can amplify the color scheme of arrangements that incorporate white, while also providing a neutral base for other colors in a design. The basket weave lends this arrangement a countrified note of casualness, making it a perfect choice for a centerpiece at an informal dinner. *Above:* The intriguing surface weave and rich coloration of this grapevine basket elevates it to the stature of being a container for elegant roses. While it lends the design an interesting texture, it is also unobtrusive enough to let the beauty of the flowers shine through.

flowers look particularly nice in baskets. Also, because of their unique qualities, baskets may have slightly irregular shapes. These irregularities may cause balance problems in the basket, particularly if it is a vertical, upright design. When selecting baskets, be particularly aware of potential balance problems by checking carefully for any wobbling. If you do end up with an irregular basket, try steaming it for three to five minutes. Then place it on a flat surface and press down with your palm until the fibers begin to yield and the unevenness is corrected. Baskets can also be weighted with small bags of sand or pebbles to keep them from toppling.

Wicker baskets, in particular, are available in many sizes and shapes. With the smooth rhythm of their weave, they act as neutral containers. When lacquered, they emphasize the smooth qualities of the flowers they contain.

Baskets fashioned from grape vines are also excellent, texture-rich containers. The many other types of fibers used are too numerous to list. New basket styles are constantly being created. Some baskets are even designed with hooks so that they function as wall hangings with flowers and greens cascading over their sides.

GLASS

Glass is another often-used container material that can take on many forms. In the past, clear glass was thought to distract from arrangements because it reveals the inner workings of an arrangement. Today, however, clear glass containers are particularly popular. Solid-colored glass marbles or exquisitely rounded stones can be added to designs to disguise their mechanics while providing beautiful accents at the same time. Today we recognize that there is an elegant simplicity to a design in which stems can clearly be seen rising from within a container.

Glass containers vary in size, shape, and mood. The first place to look for glass and/or crystal containers is in your home cabinets. Ordinary drinking glasses are versatile, satisfactory, neutral containers. The effect of a design using drinking glasses can be multiplied by the use of several glasses filled with arrangements that contrast and complement one another. Wine glasses and flutes, with their smoothly defined and often dramatic qualities, are also good choices.

Simple glass bowls, too, act as effective containers if they have some depth. A few simple magnolia blossoms, mums, or any other round flower can be nicely displayed in a low, open bowl.

Cut-crystal bowls or vases should be used for opulent arrangements of such classic flowers as roses, orchids, and lilies. Crystal bud vases are quite popular, but use lighter flowers with such delicate vases as you won't want to topple them. Ordinary beakers also make good bud vases. Small glass perfume jars or medium-size bottles also work well as containers for small-scale arrangements. The effect of such arrangements can be magnified when several bottles are used together, perhaps even set on a mirror base.

Another important aspect of glass is its ability to evoke period styles. Victorian-era green-glass battery jars and ruby-red glass can add a shimmering vitality to an arrangement, perhaps by echoing foliage or a focal color. Similar effects can be achieved with modern colored glass.

Simple yet captivating, clear glass is a remarkably effective container. When flowers are displayed in glass, they seem more vital and alive because the stems are visible and it is possible to see each flower as a whole. In this design, the stems are clearly seen inside the glass—where they are subtly anchored by glass marbles—and deliberate visual connections between the inside of the container and the outside are made with the interplay of stems and foliage.

Left: Ceramic containers are available in a vast array of colors and shapes. They are extremely effective containers because they adapt to a variety of arrangement styles and attractively camouflage the inner mechanics of a design. Here, a lavender ceramic container subtly harmonizes with the floral color scheme and provides clarification for the shape of the design. Above: Grevillea is a versatile dried arranging material and works well in any number of containers. Here it is teamed with glycerine-treated evergreen in a terra-cotta pot. The pot is cast as a double-sided lion's head and demonstrates the versatility of pottery design as well as inviting the viewer to study the arrangement from different angles.

CERAMICS & POTTERY.

The term ceramics covers many objects, all produced by heating clay. The results are earthenware (which includes pottery), stoneware, and porcelain. The glazes applied to such pieces can create varied surface finishes that will produce different effects in a design. Particularly popular today are the lacquered black, gray, and soft pastel shades of ceramics.

Ceramic container shapes vary from the sturdy block to the cylinder to long-necked and broad-based vases. They also lend themselves well to the low-bowl shape, which has so many uses. Ceramic containers are also frequently oval shaped with low bases. This shape lends itself particularly well to contemporary line designs. However, oval containers can present problems in the mechanics of arranging. The opening is generally small, while the bowl area is large. Therefore, problems arise when materials are inserted. If you wish to use an oval ceramic bowl for a design that requires precise placement of material, simply stack pieces of Styrofoam—attached by sticky tape to the container—inside the oval bowl up to just inside the opening. That way, the arranging materials will not get lost in the bowl because you will be arranging them from a higher level.

Another important ceramic medium is terra cotta. It is a lightly fired earthenware, tempered to a brownish orange that is either glazed or unglazed. Earthenware's special contribution is that its earthy coloration combines well with garden flowers and wildflowers alike. It provides a rich yet neutral coloration that seems to embody the vitality of nature.

CHOOSING A CONTAINER

The choice of containers will depend not only on your choice of flowers but also on the decor of your home. If your furnishings are contemporary, ceramic cylinders in neutral colors will be complementary additions. These vases also combine well with traditional and Oriental schemes. You should purchase them in different heights, generally ranging from a half-foot to a foot.

Round containers make good accompaniments to casual, loose designs of short-stemmed flowers. Low bowls in neutral colors make excellent containers for ikebana and minimal designs. Deeper bowls can convey the graciousness of traditional design or can be juxtaposed with interesting angles and asymmetrical triangles to create high-tech arrangements.

Elaborate designs sometimes need the complement of more ornate containers. Footed compotes, silver and silver-plated bowls, epergnes, urns, and Victorian-style jardinieres all convey the air of the antique and are well suited to complex compositions.

Of course, a multitude of containers can be found around any household. Tins, bowls, pitchers, teapots, and serving trays from the kitchen can be dressed up in flower designs. Wooden salad bowls are another possibility and would contribute very nicely to a just-picked garden arrangement.

Such unlikely choices as oversized cylindrical umbrella stands, tall glass spaghetti canisters, or even disguised tin cans (covered with leaves or cloth) can work well as containers.

One final aspect of containers that should be considered is knowing when to incorporate a pedestal or base. Some particularly regal designs benefit from the addition of a pedestal such as a piece of lacquered wood or a slab of marble. Be sure that the addition of such bases does not overpower the design to make it look too heavily rooted.

Other possibilities are Oriental mats, trays, plastic picture frames with a fabric inserted under the plastic that harmonizes with the color scheme, or mirrors, which echo the design. The addition of a base can contribute many qualities to a design. It can provide a contrast of form, for example, by offsetting a vertical container with a horizontal line. Bases also reinforce the unity of color and texture and create more depth by drawing the eye into the arrangement and then back to the base. Adding a base can also introduce the illusion of space in the arrangement by elevating a design.

A low ceramic bowl is the traditional holder for Oriental designs. The choice of white for the bowl is particularly appropriate here, because it acts as a neutral base that also complements the white of the flowers. Such bowls are also inexpensive and readily available from specialty and floral-supply stores. Low ceramic bowls can also host a variety of designs that are not Orientally influenced.

BO PARKER

47

Above: A low bowl places greater emphasis on the flowers in the design. Therefore, the colors and positioning of the flowers requires special attention. In this design, lilies, calla lilies, irises, freesia, and tuberoses create just the right balance. **Right:** Clear glass containers suggest the unlimited possibilities of flower design. Here, blue agapanthus, pink alstroemeria, goldenrod, filler flowers, and branches are combined boldly in an arrangement that freely extends upward from its base. The use of dramatic agapanthus with the common goldenrod exemplifies an important aspect of contemporary design: use of surprisingly varied materials. The modern glass container further emphasizes this aspect.

FRESH FLOWER CONTAINERS

For fresh flower designs, glass, plastic, and pottery or ceramics are very good choices because they take well to water and flower preservatives. When metal comes into contact with flower preservatives, it tends to corrode. Such containers are also easy to clean, with a solution of detergent and chlorine bleach or a traditional mixture of lemon juice and salt.

If you simply must use metal for a fresh flower arrangement, either line the container with aluminum foil or place a small bowl inside to hold the water and camouflage this with greens extending over the sides of the arrangement. This way, the container is protected from discoloration or corrosion.

When using clear glass containers with fresh flowers, keep the water clean at all times or it will spoil the effect. Slightly tinted glass is an alternative that requires less maintenance.

Don't think that because fresh flowers require water, porous containers such as baskets or clay flowerpots cannot be used. Simply place a plastic container of water or well-soaked floral foam covered with plastic on the inside to separate the water from the container.

DRIED FLOWER CONTAINERS

Just as ideas about suitable containers for fresh flowers have changed, so have ideas about possibilities for dried flowers. Contrary to what many people believe, clear glass can be used for everlastings arrangements. Strong, dramatic materials such as heliconia, bittersweet, and bamboo do not need the support of foam and look absolutely breathtaking when casually arranged in a cylindrical glass container, perhaps weighted with some stones. Ruby glass and other colored glasses also make fine containers for everlastings designs. Spanish moss can be tucked in around the foam base to further obscure the mechanics.

Baskets, in particular, are appropriate for dried flower designs. Because they are made of natural materials, they are the traditional holders for dried flowers. And because everlastings do not need water, there is no danger of harming the basket.

Earthy-looking pottery and terracotta pieces are also natural containers for everlastings, whose autumnal colors harmonize naturally with them. However, dried arrangements need not be relegated to the realm of the informal. Classic arrangements using rounded forms and stunningly preserved greens are worthy of ornate containers.

Whether you are using low bowls for ikebana-related dried designs, high-tech black cylinders for arrangements using unusual pods and other striking forms, or simply a slab of driftwood up and around which the design is built, containers for everlastings reflect the liberating qualities of these dried design materials. Because they do not require water, and because you do not even have to create the illusion that they are fresh, everlastings arrangements can be added to any container and sometimes do not actually require one.

One last thing to remember is that everlastings designs topple easily, so the containers may need to be weighted with stones, bags of sand, pebbles, or other objects.

Left: Since everlastings do not require water, baskets are their natural home. A low, open basket such as this one displays rarely obtainable colored statice in a casual and natural-looking way. *Right top:* Dried flowers lend themselves naturally to a number of unusual containers. Here, a dried crown gourd provides a charming base for a grouping of bright orange strawflowers and a palm frond. *Right bottom:* Dried gourds work well with earth-toned materials. The burnt umber pine cones, dusty green hakea, and lavender-gray tears-of-the-Madonna pods used in this design extend the subtle coloration of the container itself, making it a very appropriate arrangement for autumn.

TONY CENICOLA

TONY CENICOLA

ARTIFICIAL FLOWER CONTAINERS

Left: Silver bowls, particularly footed ones, are not only appropriate for formal designs, but also are eye-catching containers for wildflowers arranged in an artful fashion. This design uses the sleek qualities of artificial flowers to best advantage, blending their delicate textures with the lustrous smoothness of the silver bowl. The traditional triangular design, surprisingly carried out with novel flowers, is punctuated elegantly by pink liatris spikes, which seem to echo the footed base of the container. Above: Although baskets usually play a textural role in a design, they can also contribute decorative motifs. Here, a sprightly pastel-painted basket not only contributes texture and a lovely open form in which to display the artificial daisies, but also adds a new dimension of color and suggests the presence of other flowers.

Because, like everlastings, artificial flowers do not require water, your imagination is the only restriction when considering the range of containers that can be used with them.

Clear and colored glass of all shapes and sizes can freely be used with artificial flowers. So, too, can pottery and ceramic containers as well as baskets. In fact, baskets can be used with even greater freedom because artificial flowers can be massed in artful groupings—without fear of breakage, as with everlastings—and without any water.

Valuable silver bowls and other metal containers can be used without the fear of damaging the metal. Artificial flowers can be used in compositions that do not require a formal container: Pieces of driftwood, charming carved wooden boxes, and a multitude of other objects can be freely used.

ARRANGING FRESH FLOWERS

The ultimate measure of success for a flower arrangement is how long it lasts. Because you want the life of fresh arrangements to last, it is absolutely vital that you know how to select the freshest flowers and know how to keep them fresh for as long as possible. All too often, people buy flowers hastily and plunk them into a vase of water without giving any thought to how the flowers will maintain their vitality. By taking a few minutes to examine leaves, branches, and petals at the florist and by preconditioning the flowers before arranging, it is possible to dramatically alter nature's course.

SELECTING

Whether picking flowers from the garden or selecting them from the florist, certain criteria for flower choice must be applied. When selecting flowers at the florist's, look for those that have petals facing upward toward the center. The petals should not be marred by bruises or folds; the flower heads should not droop or bend at the neck; and the petals should be firm, with strong, unfaded colors. Signs of opaqueness in the flower petals can be a sign of age, and white spots indicate prolonged refrigeration. It is impossible to generalize about flower coloration and its relationship to age because each flower has different qualities. If you are aware of what the optimum color of the flower should be, compare it with the flower's present color. If the color around the edges of the petals seems too dark or the color of the flower is significantly

lighter, this is probably a sign that the flower is not fresh.

By looking at the center of a flower, you can also tell its age. If the centers have advanced to the seed stage—that is, there is a build-up of pollen—the flower is in the process of completing its reproductive cycle and will not last long in an arrangement. It's preferable to choose flowers that are just beginning to open so you can enjoy the full flowering stage of the blossom. While it is possible that the flowers may bloom if the buds are tightly shut, you run the risk of the flowers not opening at all. Some flowers, however, can generally be counted on to bloom into full flower in bud stage. Among these flowers are roses, gladiolus, and tulips.

Another important aspect of the flower to check is the condition of the leaves and stems. Leaves that are yellowed, spotted, or drooping are a sure sign of age. Any discoloration or visible build-up of bacteria around the stems is an indication that the plant is past its prime.

When selecting flowers from the garden, do not choose flowers either too early or too late in their cycles. You do not want to stunt a bud's growth, nor do you want to choose a flower that will fade quickly once brought indoors. Pick them either in the beginning of the day, when the buds are just beginning to open, or in the early evening, when their food stores are at their peak. Never pick flowers at midday because their moisture content is very low at this time. Make your cuts on a slant, and get the flowers into water immediately. More information on keeping flowers fresh is provided on page 56.

BO PARKER

*Left: The pristine beauty of these white and pink-tinged roses and hydrangea blooms exemplifies the qualities to look for when selecting cut flowers. Crisp, smooth petals and firm, green foliage indicate that the arranging materials are fresh. **Above:** The freshness of the flowers used in this arrangement is evident not only through the vibrant colors of the petals but also through their upright, vivacious forms. The use of a few lilies with closed buds ensures the continuation of the life of the arrangement.*

KEEPING FLOWERS FRESH

Once you've chosen the flowers for the arrangement you envision, preconditioning them increases their longevity. When a flower's stem is cut, it is separated from its roots, through which it receives food and water. The stem attempts to heal itself by sealing the end with a kind of callus. However, when the end of the stem is sealed, it is not possible to get water and nutrients to the flower. To prevent stems from sealing themselves off, precondition them with these steps:

1. Place flowers horizontally in about 6 inches of clean water at room temperature so they will be completely covered. With an extremely sharp knife or shears, make a cut 1 or 2 inches from the bottom of the stem at a 45-degree angle while the flowers are underwater. Making the cut while the flowers are submerged ensures that an airlock will not form in the stem, thus blocking the flow of water to the flower. Also, making the cut at an angle exposes the maximum number of cells on the stem to the water. The diagonal cut also ensures that stems will not rest directly on the bottom of the container, so that access to water will not be blocked.

2. Leave the flowers in the water for at least 30 minutes, but preferably for an hour or longer. During this time they should show signs of reviving, but if they don't, recut the stems an inch higher up. Leave them in the water for at least 30 minutes more, until they begin to perk up.

3. With the knife or shears, remove foliage that will rest below the waterline in the arrangement. These leaves will promote bacterial growth if left on the stems. If there is an abundance of leaves above the waterline, pare these down too as you don't want the leaves to draw water before it can get to the flowers. The same rule applies to roses; remove the thorns that fall below the waterline.

4. Transfer the flowers into the container you will be using for your arrangement. Half fill the container with warm water and add either flower preservative according to the product's directions or 2 drops of chlorine bleach and a little sugar, which provides the necessary glucose for the flowers. Adding one or two aspirin cuts down on water loss. Some experts recommend other additives such as natural charcoal, alcohol, vinegar, or a solution of 1 part salt, 1 part potassium chloride, 4 parts alum, and 6 parts glucose added to 1 part water.

5. Place the container in a cool spot, away from direct sunlight, for one hour. Then you are ready to arrange following the suggestions in Chapter 7. Do not add more life-preserving ingredients during the life of the arrangement, but do change the water regularly, preferably every day. If possible, mist the arrangement regularly from above. Also important is placing the arrangement out of drafts and out of direct sun.

These basic steps apply to all flowers, but certain flowers have special needs. After being cut, bulb flowers have a white substance on the ends of the stems that should be snipped off to prevent nutrient blockage. Daffodils, narcissus, and hyacinths produce a milky white fluid when their stems are cut. Therefore, after these flowers are cut, they should stand out of water until they stop leaking this substance. This should take about a half hour. Then, place the flowers in warm water for an hour to allow the remainder of the substance to wash away. Do not recut the stems after this. The flowers are now ready.

BO PARKER

BO PARKER

Left: *The use of a clear glass container requires that flowers be kept as fresh as possible to eliminate filminess in the vase. This arrangement of tulips, lilies, and smartweed is camouflaged with moss so that all attention is focused on the vibrant color contrasts of the flowers.* **Above:** *This lively arrangement maintains its freshness through preconditioning. The lilies were purchased in the bud stage for longer-lasting flowers. To ensure prolonged life of all the flowers as well as an uncrowded fit into the vase, foliage that would have rested below the waterline was removed.*

Flowers with hollow stems, such as amaryllis, large dahlias, delphiniums, and lupines also require special treatment. It is especially difficult for water to make it to the flower head in hollow stems, so these flowers should be turned upside down and filled with water. Seal the end of each stem with your thumb and place the flower in the water.

Other plants may need extra measures to be revived. Imported exotic flowers that have lost some of their freshness in their long journeys from exotic locales should be laid, submerged, in a pan of water for about twenty minutes after being cut underwater. Violets and magnolias sometimes also require submersion in water, for an hour. Greens—except for the silver-, gray-, and wooly-leaved varieties—benefit from long, cool soaking in water overnight.

Left: It is particularly important to maintain optimal freshness for flowers in bridal bouquets like this one. The preconditioning process is extremely important with bouquets, which require the freshest flowers possible because they are separated from water. The beauty of the dendrobium orchids, anemones, and waxflowers demonstrates the success of preconditioning.
Below: Keeping a design fresh in a low bowl is possible through two basic methods: the use of water-soaked floral foam and positioning a water-filled, cup-shaped pinholder. Camouflage can be achieved through the use of greens, Spanish moss and other mosses, pebbles, glass marbles, or any other imaginative base cover that comes to mind.

This varied arrangement needs little more than a profusion of flowers to be held together, the framework of branches providing a natural base for the design. The freshness of the flowers is shown off to best advantage by the use of a clear glass bowl. Additionally, the arrangement of the flowers themselves—in an outwardly reaching form that compels the viewer to enjoy their fragrances up close—is particularly well suited to the naturally drooping forms of fresh-cut blooms.

WORKING WITH FRESH FLOWERS

You will need to have special tools and materials on hand in order to have the freedom to create a number of different arrangement styles. While a few striking flowers added to a clear vase requires few other tools and materials than a sharp knife and some flower preservative, creating a design filled with many components will no doubt require more tools.

A few of the basic items you need to have on hand include a sharp knife, such as a florist's knife, for cutting flower stems (the blade should be no longer than 6 inches); shears for cutting branches and wires; and a few tall and short buckets and basins to hold the flowers in while they are being preconditioned. Other basic items needed are containers, cut-flower food, and a plastic spray bottle for misting flowers.

Also important to have on hand are a range of aids for holding flowers in place. Among the simplest to use are clear-glass and colored-glass marbles, which do not have to be hidden from view. Also attractive are small rounded stones and black Oriental pebbles.

Another device, the pinholder, is a very effective way of holding flowers. Pinholders range in shape from round to square to rectangular. They contain a number of evenly spaced pins upon which flowers are inserted. The cup-shaped ones actually hold water, which makes it possible to use fresh flowers in a porous container, such as a basket, because the water is isolated from the container.

BO PARKER

60

Floral foam is an effective and adaptable choice for holding fresh flowers in place. Not only does floral foam hold the flowers in place, but it also supplies them with water because it is highly absorbent. Because it is green, floral foam also acts as a camouflaging agent, blending in with the arrangement. It can be further camouflaged with the addition of greens, such as galax or ivy, and mosses, including Spanish moss. A knife can be used to cut floral foam to fit the size of the container. You may wish to leave about an inch of floral foam extending beyond the edge of the container so that you will have greater freedom angling your fresh material into the right positions.

Sometimes floral foam needs to be held in place with waterproof tape—not the same thing as florist's tape—which comes in several colors and in a clear form. To anchor the

Left: These delicate, fresh, yellow freesia convey their vitality not only through their vibrant coloration but also through their natural placement in the vase. A ceramic vase with a narrow neck such as this one allows for free use of mechanics to hold flowers in place because the anchoring device is hidden. *Below:* This lovely ikebana arrangement is lent a tropical air with the flaming red heliconia and the evocatively shaped anthuriums. The striking clear glass marbles disguise the mechanics of the arrangement.

To create this traditional corsage of six dendrobium orchids, remove the stems and wire each flower calyx to a number 22–23 gauge wire and cover with floral tape. Gather all of the wires together and cover the join with floral tape, allowing numerous layers for stability in the corsage. Bend the flowers into place. If you wish to add ribbon, gather a silky, lustrous variety into graceful folds and join it with tape to the wire stem.

foam with the tape, soak the foam in water and place it in an empty container. Run two crisscrossed pieces of tape over the top of the foam and secure the ends to the sides of the container. Camouflage with foliage or moss.

Among other items for holding fresh flowers in place are chicken wire, which can be cut to the shape of the container, and a new and useful item called Iglu™. This is a plastic igloo-shaped cage in which floral foam is contained.

Aside from manipulating fresh flowers through holders, you can both strengthen and lengthen flowers by using floral wire, picks, and tapes. Wire, which comes in different weights called *gauges,* can fortify and lengthen stems. The higher the gauge number, the lighter the wire. Number 22 gauge is a good wire to work with for most fresh flowers.

To wire a flower, cut a piece of wire that is as long as you wish the stem to be and pierce it through the calyx (the bottom of the blossom head, which acts as a cup for the petals). Wrap it around the calyx a few times and then bring it down the stem. To lengthen a stem, you can use either prewired florist's picks or the unwired variety. Attach these to the base of the stem with wire. They range in size from three to six inches.

To cover up the joins made by the wires and picks, you can use florist's tape, which is available in a wide variety of colors. In general, match the tape with the color of the stem or branch. When using the tape, start just under the flower head and wrap it around two times. Then, roll the stem into the tape, which should be held out tautly. It is easy to break it off at the end with your hands. Do not wrap the tape too tightly or cover the end of the flower as you will cut off its circulation.

BO PARKER

ARRANGING DRIED FLOWERS

The possibilities for creating exciting displays with dried flowers are limitless. The range of colors that everlastings come in is indeed wide and enthusiasm for them is increasing. Everlastings displays are being more widely seen in public spaces, such as restaurants and lobbies, because interior designers recognize that these arrangements require little maintenance and provide stunning and long-lasting results with tremendous aesthetic appeal.

However, although dried arrangements require little maintenance, this does not mean that dried plants do not require special care. Everlastings do not have the resiliency of fresh flowers; they tend to be brittle and have often traveled long distances from such diverse places as Australia, Africa, and South America to arrive at your florist's shop. They need extra care in storing, in handling, and in your working with them.

GATHERING AND COLLECTING

When buying everlastings at the florist, check very carefully to make sure that the flowers are not loose and that the stems are not broken. If they are wrapped in solid-colored paper, simply pick up the bag and hold it upside down, giving it a very light shake. There is liable to be some spillage from the bag, but if excessive amounts of petals fall out, you know the contents of the package have been damaged in shipping. Make sure, too, that the pods are not crushed and the leaves are not torn.

If you choose to gather everlastings in the wild, first obtain a list of endangered species from your local U.S.D.A. Conservation Service so that you don't inadvertently do harm to what nature has to offer. Second, obtain a good field guide that will help you identify the different plants and will also help you avoid potentially unpleasant situations, such as picking poisonous, deadly, and life-endangering plants. If you are unsure about what flowers will achieve the look you want when dried, *Everlastings* (Facts On File) is a fine reference that illustrates a wide variety of dried flowers in a catalog format.

Equip yourself with some basic tools. Bring a secateur, or pruning shears, as well as a medium-size lopper for branches. A pocketknife is also very useful. It will help you cut some of the thinner stems as well as strip unwanted foliage and thorns from plants. Take along a large bucket in which you can submerge flowers and foliage that would otherwise wilt on the journey home. You might also wish to put foliage, ferns, or herbs in sealed plastic bags filled with water. Seed pods and other fragile plants can be wrapped in newspaper.

When gathering everlastings, never remove a plant from the ground by its roots. Cut stems and branches cleanly. Do not select flowers that are growing alone in a location. If you are collecting seed pods, shake the seeds free from them so that the plant can regenerate.

Prime locations to gather everlastings are nearby brooks,

Left: An unusual combination of materials—air-dried mimosa and evergreens—spills over the sides of an attractively designed shopping bag. Since everlastings do not require water, a vast variety of objects can serve effectively—and surprisingly well—as containers. *Above:* Many line forms are at work in this fascinating dried design, which is united by the monochromatic brown color scheme. Spiky cattails, dried flowers, and seedpods seem to be propelled out of the swirling form of the basket container. Round everlastings, some with touches of white, provide contrast in the design, while a realistic touch of green at the base makes the arrangement look as if it is growing out of a forest floor.

67

streams, or any wetland areas. A wide variety of grasses, pods, sedges, rushes, and other beautiful plants that are stunning in dried form abound in these areas. Wood edges and meadows are also excellent locations for finding potential everlastings.

As with picking flowers for fresh arrangements, do not pick plant materials at midday, when their moisture content is lowest. It is helpful to bind materials in loose bunches as you collect them, and you should spray them with insecticide to avoid potential problems.

When gathering garden flowers or choosing fresh florist's flowers for everlastings arrangements, select the freshest, most blemish-free specimens available. The beauty in the fresh flower is captured and reflected in the dried flower. However, any flaws and blemishes on petals and leaves will be magnified in the drying process. Therefore, it is vital that the flower starts off as perfect-looking as possible.

AN OVERVIEW OF DRYING METHODS

Although everlastings are now widely available in stores, it is still a very rewarding home activity to dry flowers. There are five basic drying methods you can use and different types are applicable to different flowers and foliage. Whichever methods you choose, it's a good idea to set aside workroom and storage area for such tasks.

Before you begin drying, make sure that the materials you plan to use, both plants and tools, are completely dry. Also, it's a good idea to dry more flowers than you will need to leave room for error should any flowers become damaged or dry poorly. You can store these extras in layers of tissue paper in boxes in your workroom.

Of course, many plant materials do not really need to be dried very much at all. Keep pods, berries, branches, and other such material upright in containers until you are ready to use them. These can actually lend sculptural accents around the home while they are drying, so mass them loosely in containers in places where they can be seen but will not be damaged.

One of the easiest drying methods is *air drying*. It can be used effectively for a wide variety of material and produces excellent results. Start with a dark, dry, dust-free room in which there is good ventilation. You do not want the flowers to dry as a result of sunlight, which fades colors. Plan to air dry flowers as soon as possible after they are picked. Drying plants as quickly as possible helps to permanently capture their lovely qualities.

If you are air drying flowers, you will most likely want to remove any foliage from the plants. Take a small bunch of flowers and tie them with a string. The bunch shouldn't have any more than twenty or so flowers because you don't want to squeeze them together in the drying process. It's a good idea, too, to cut the stems at different lengths so that the flower heads can dry naturally without pressing against one another and distorting their shapes. Prepare a number of bunches to be dried.

Hang them to dry from hooks, hangers, string, chicken wire, dowels, or any other type of holder. The best effects are generally produced from hanging them upside down. However, you may not want to dry all your materials this way. Let grasses, rushes, and other foliage that can take a snaky,

An arangement of silica-dried roses comes to life because of the careful positioning of the flowers. The roses are situated at different heights in the design, creating a smooth sense of rhythm. Lacy air-dried gypsophila and German statice provide wispy accents.

A scarlet container sets the tone for the dried materials it contains. Red-dyed ruscus leaves delight the eye and create a riveting focal point. Ruscus can be air dried or treated with glycerine. Dramatic, sculptural sweeps of honey locusts, velvetlike dried petals of the king protea, and catalpa pods create a sense of movement equal to the impact of the red color.

curvaceous shape air dry in vases. They will add immeasurably to an arrangement. Some material dries better horizontally, attached loosely by string or hung loosely to a dowel or other kind of hanger. In this way, the material is free to develop more evocative curves and will twist more as it dries. Depending on the type of plant and its bulkiness and moisture-retaining qualities, air drying can take from three to five weeks.

A variation on the air-drying method is the *evaporation technique.* Using this method, plants stand in 2 inches of water until they are dry. This method takes slightly longer than air drying, but the flowers and greens retain more of their natural curves this way.

Another method of drying flowers is the *sand/borax technique.* This process results in more natural-looking dried flowers because they are dried without any exposure to air or light. Begin by obtaining a shoe box or stationery box with enough room to hold the flowers so that they do not touch each other as they are drying.

Obtain a quantity of very fine dust- and silt-free sand. The sand should not have any salt in it, so if you are using beach sand, wash and dry it completely before use. Alternately, you can use a mixture of 1 part borax to 3 to 4 parts cornmeal.

Add 2 inches of sand or the borax mixture to the box. If the flowers you will be drying have a simple, single-petaled structure, such as daisies, dry them face down. After you have

70

A touch of the American Southwest is conveyed through this intriguing design of woody-stemmed everlastings, which come predried in this snaky form. The similarly colored container, with its maze of motifs, helps carry through the monochromatic design. An undulating Mexican serape backdrop completes the ensemble.

added the flowers to the box so that they completely cover the surface but do not touch one another, gently cover them with 2 more inches of the mixture, slowly adding it so that there are no lumps. Gently shake the box as you add the sand or borax to ensure that the mixture is evenly distributed among the flower petals. The stems can stick out of the mixture, and you should not cover the box. Allow it to sit undisturbed for three to five weeks.

Drying time depends on the bulk of the flowers and on the humidity of the atmosphere. You can check on the process after three weeks by uncovering one flower. If the material needs more drying time, bury it again and check it in a few days to a week, depending on how advanced the drying process was. Dry only one type of flower in a box so you can keep accurate track of the drying time that is required.

For those flowers with bulky stems that will not dry easily, it is best to remove the stems before drying and replace them with wire. Use a 6- to 8-inch piece of 24- to 21-gauge wire for most flowers. A heavier weight can be used for particularly large specimens. To wire a flower, leave a 1-inch stem on the flower and insert the wire up through the stem. Be sure not to stick the wire up through the head of the flower. For flowers with hollow stems, simply stick the wire through the stem. For flowers with woody, hard stems, you can wire the flower through the calyx. You might also want to do this when the flower stem is very thin.

71

TONY CENICOLA

Above: An exotic doll bride from India holds a bouquet of silica-dried marigolds and German statice, demonstrating everlastings' ability to be displayed in a variety of ways. The golden color of her trailing ribbon enhances the warm tones of the flowers. *Right:* Dried golden mushrooms and ruscus and camellia leaves top a straw hat with surprising results. Earthy-looking and reminiscent of flower shapes, this mushroom variety transforms the hat into a unique display item or fun fashion accessory. Note how the similarly colored foliage adds texture to the design and creates a transition for the green ribbon.

Flowers with more complex petal structures, or those that have cupped petals or upright shapes, must be dried upright in the sand or borax mixture. These flowers must be wired before drying. After you have wired them, simply add 2 inches of drying mixture or sand to the box. Sharply bend the wired stems where they join with the natural stems so that the flowers can be placed face up and the stems will bend upward. Add more sand or borax mixture, shaking the box gently to ensure that all petals are covered.

Those flowers that grow on long stalks should be placed lengthwise in a drying container. The same steps are followed, with extra care taken to evenly distribute the drying medium.

When removing dried flowers from their drying containers, remember to do so gently. First, uncover one flower to see if it is dried. Remove it gently from the drying medium. To excavate the others, tilt the box to one side and slowly pour out the sand or borax mixture. As the flowers begin to appear, simply lift them out.

The same general technique is used for the *silica gel method,* although it takes much less time for the material to dry and the box must be sealed tightly. The time needed to dry flowers in this medium varies from two to ten days, depending on the bulkiness of the flower. Truly lifelike color can be produced with this drying method. Flowers are prepared in the same way as are those dried in sand or borax mixture (see page 70). Freesia and ranunculus, in particular, benefit greatly from being dried in silica gel.

Left: A stunning dried design of white branches, statice, pearly white everlastings, filler flowers, and eucalyptus is surprisingly colorful for a dried arrangement. Above: Red roses, German statice, heather, and pussy willow each contribute a contrasting texture and form to this expressive dried arrangement. The materials require different drying techniques: roses should be dried with silica gel but can also be bought predried; delphinium and statice air dry easily; and pussy willow simply air dries while displayed in the arrangement. The basket's subtly interwoven design echoes the arrangement itself, which radiates smoothly and seamlessly from the center.

Although flowers are generally the mainstay of any arrangement, foliage, too, makes an important contribution in any design. The *glycerine method* is used to dry foliage, and it often produces stunning results. Many types of foliage, such as eucalyptus, leucanthoe, papyrus, and ruscus, are sold pretreated with glycerine. When using this method at home, use only fresh foliage picked in midseason.

Small, single leaves not on branches should be submerged in a half-water, half-glycerine solution for two to three weeks. To create interesting variations, you can try removing the leaves at different intervals. Leaves react in different ways when submerged in glycerine. Some turn gray, while others take on a bronzed look, and still others become striated with many different colors running through them.

For entire branches, cut a 3- or 4-inch incision in the bottom of the stem. Put the branches in a solution of 1 part glycerine with 2 or 3 parts near-boiling water. Leave the branches to sit in the solution for two to six weeks, depending on the density of the branches. You'll know the process is done when the leaves turn colors and become extremely flexible.

A time-honored method of preserving flowers and greens is through *pressing*. Although the dried flowers that result from pressing are primarily used in pressed picture designs, pressed foliage can be used in a variety of ways in arrangements. Ferns, juniper, gladiolus leaves, and many other types of naturally flat foliage take well to the pressing process.

You can approach pressing through three methods. You can use a traditional flower press or a heavy book, both of which methods will produce very flat, one-dimensional results. Or you can use layers of newspaper, which works particularly well for drying foliage to produce more natural-looking results.

First of all, choose a warm, dry place to press your materials. Also, since pressing generally takes two weeks or longer, you will want to do your pressing in an out-of-the-way place, where the material will not be disturbed.

To use a flower press, simply follow the instructions that accompany it. Such flower presses have alternating layers of wood and blotting paper. Pressure is applied by the tightening of nuts.

The book method allows many layers of plant material to be dried simultaneously. Any large, heavy book, such as a phone book, is good for this purpose. Simply place a piece of untextured tissue paper or paper towel on one side of the pages of an opened book. Place the material to be dried on the paper. If you are drying flowers, you can leave the stems on the flowers if they are not heavy. Otherwise, remove the stems and dry them separately. If you do remove the stems, leave about one-quarter of an inch of the stem on each flower so that it can be picked up easily. Add a second sheet of paper over the drying material. If you wish, add a bookmark so you can easily find where you placed your material. You can create many layers using this process. Close the book and place another one of about the same weight on top of it. After two weeks, check to see if the plants are dried. If not, allow them to sit for another week.

To use the newspaper method, simply spread a few sheets of newspaper on a flat surface and add a few leaves so that they are not touching one another. Add more sheets of newspaper and another layer of foliage. As with the book method, you can build up a few layers this way.

STORING DRIED FLOWERS

After you've dried your flowers, you need to put them away in a safe place because they are so delicate. To store dried flowers, it is generally best to lay them horizontally in large, labeled boxes. Delicate pieces should be wrapped in clear plastic wrapping paper or in tissue paper. Do not put too many different kinds of flowers in one box so that you avoid confusion and unnecessary handling. If they are to be stored for a long period of time, bunches of flowers or greens can be covered with tissue paper and hung from ceiling racks or chicken wire.

Flowers and greens can also be temporarily stored upright in glass vases or even set aside in Styrofoam or strung through chicken wire. Glycerine-treated foliage can be wrapped in layers of newspaper; air-dried pods and grasses should be stored in plastic bags or sheets. Silica-dried flowers should not be stored in this medium: Pack them in air-tight tins or in boxes. Flowers dried in sand or borax can be left in these

*Below: Everlastings often surpass the beauty of fresh flowers as their unusual dried forms contribute a dramatic intensity to a design. The heliconia plant used in this grouping demonstrates the unusual twists into which dried flowers form—the flowers take approximately two to three weeks to air dry. Strelitzia leaves add a dimension of curved complexity to the design, whose form is elongated by a straight black vase. **Right:** Dried gladiola leaves, bear grass, and iris pods combine to recreate the simple beauty of the outdoors in this relaxed, oversized arrangement. Perfect for an autumn display in an entryway or dining room, this arrangement requires only a basic understanding of flower design to create. The materials radiate from the highest point in the center and spill over the sides in a scaled yet natural-looking profusion. All materials used air dry easily. The foliage was covered lightly with green floral spray and then lightly dusted with gold floral spray.*

TONY CENICOLA

TONY CENICOLA

Jack-o-lanterns are distinctively sculptural dried plants that need very minimal accompaniment. In this design, a horseshoe-shaped basket acts as a partial container. The jack-o-lantern is among the most vibrantly colored autumn plants and only requires air drying for use.

media until they are used. Otherwise, they should also be packed in air-tight tins or in boxes. Branches don't need to be stored with the same care as flowers. They can be stored upright anywhere around the house in containers.

WORKING WITH DRIED FLOWERS

Everlastings require specialized tools and materials in order for the arranger to achieve the most effective results. Like fresh flowers, dried flowers require certain basic tools. You will already have purchased a florist's knife and shears for cutting stems, branches, and wire; because everlastings require a lot of wiring, you might also want to have a wire cutter on hand. Styrofoam, which you will also be using, may necessitate the purchase of a small saw to cut through this material. Tweezers,

too, are an important everlastings arranging tool, because their fine tips are needed for picking up delicate arranging materials and for getting into tight spaces.

Other basics, which are also staples for fresh flowers, that are needed for working with everlastings are wire, florist's tape in a variety of colors, and wired and unwired wooden picks. In addition, sticky tape, which comes in large rolls of white and green, is quite useful because it adheres on both sides and is good for affixing to Styrofoam.

Like fresh flowers, everlastings need to be held in place in a design. For this purpose, a number of different holders are employed. The most common material used is green Styrofoam, which is available in slab form and is cut in blocks to fit the size of the container. Brown foam is also used, and it is

Strawflowers are the focal flowers in the lower left corner of this arrangement. Spikes of purplish liatris shift and focus from round shapes to linear forms and carry the viewer's eye around the design. Other spots of secondary color are contributed by the yellow morrism, red cherry peppers, and orange capsicum fruit, which shrivels when dried. The asymmetry of the design echoes the shape of the pitcher container.

available in brick form. Brown foam is easier to work with because it is softer than Styrofoam, but sticky tape does not adhere to its surface so that glue must be used to hold the brown foam in place. A third kind of foam called Bar-Fast™ is also available in brick form and comes sealed in plastic bags because it is moist. Neither glue nor tape can be used with this type of foam, and it must therefore be cut to the exact dimensions of the container. As it dries, this kind of foam locks around the stems to hold the materials tightly in place. Yet another option for anchoring materials is Sahara,™ which is available in brick form and should be fitted tightly to the container. You can use glue to hold it in place. It is very easy to work with, although it is slightly denser than brown foam. As with fresh flowers, pinholders and marbles can also be used.

A number of other items should be purchased for greater versatility in working with everlastings. Fast-drying white or clear glue is quite useful for repairing broken stems or tucking flowers into a specific place. Watercolors will help touch up faded colors in a design. Spray paints in various shades can also help transform everlastings by imparting dramatic shades. Fine- and medium-size paintbrushes are used with the watercolors on both petals and leaves. Polyurethane lacquer adds glossy highlights to a design, and flower preservatives protect flowers from moisture and dirt.

Using these basic tools and materials, it will be possible to work easily and professionally with everlastings. Remember to handle them gently at all times because they do not have the resiliency of their fresh counterparts.

ARRANGING ARTIFICIAL FLOWERS

JOHN DEANE

The popularity of artificial flowers is greater than it has ever been because of the development of fine, realistic-looking fabrics. In the past, artificial flowers were created from such diverse materials as beads, feathers, shells, and paper. Today, we can still experiment in these media, but the most popular and convincing styles are made of fabrics from polyester blends to silk. The many subtleties of color and style now available create stunning facsimiles of flowers, foliage, trees, and evergreens that are being used more and more frequently in arrangements. Though they can be relatively expensive to buy, artificial flowers are actually a bargain in the long run because their lifelike colors and forms will far outlive their fresh counterparts. Whether they are used to add variety to fresh arrangements or to provide bright spots of color on their own, artificial flowers are truly significant tools of the arranger's art.

SELECTING
While you don't have to worry about freshness when choosing artificial flowers, you must of course be aware of the quality of the blooms you are considering. Are the ends finished in as lifelike a manner as possible? Is the color gradation from petal to petal a subtle and convincing one? It is worth spending a little more money on artificial flowers that simulate nature as closely as possible?

It is a good idea to have a basic stock of artificial flowers on hand for use with all your arrangements, whether the arrange-

ment will be composed of primarily fresh, dried, or artificial flowers. There are some basic standbys that you should purchase for year-round use because they can be employed in a variety of arrangement styles, acting as both focal flowers and as supporting flowers. Among these flowers are roses, carnations, dahlias, daisies, lilacs, lilies, anemones, snapdragons, Queen Anne's lace, forget-me-nots, larkspur, chrysanthemums, violets, poppies, and antirrhinums. For example, chrysanthemums look as exciting with holly branches at holiday time as they do with tulips and buttercups in a spring bouquet. Lilies work well in both period and contemporary arrangements and combine effectively with a variety of flowers.

Having as many of these basic flower types on hand as possible will afford you a greater range of choices and will also, no doubt, inspire you to work more creatively with flowers.

FREEDOM AND DIVERSITY OF DESIGN
One of the most liberating aspects of designing with artificial flowers is that they do not require the kind of extensive preparation that fresh and dried flowers need before they can be used in an arrangement. Also, because they are so resilient, artificial flowers can be manipulated into a number of dramatic positions. The arranger need not fear handling the flowers because they might break or worry that the stems need to be placed in water.

Another wonderful aspect of artificial designs is that they can be placed in a greater variety of places than can designs

*Left: Having a supply of artificial flowers on hand makes it possible to vary designs the year round. In this case, soft-pink roses and charming forget-me-nots provide a nice foundation for a design incorporating elegantine, sweet peas, and orchids. Additionally, having a collection of baskets to vary in arrangements provides unlimited freedom in arranging because they can be painted with various motifs in different colors. **Above:** This arrangement, clearly inspired by minimal Oriental designs, reveals the remarkable possibilities for arranging with artificial flowers. The stems and foliage are easily bent into smoothly curving shapes, and because the flowers are artificial, they will hold their elegant poses throughout the life of the design.*

JOHN DEANE

Left: Elegant lotus blossoms flanked by two upward-reaching bulbs look so lifelike and serene that they seem to be floating on calm waters. The unparalleled grace of this flower calls for it to be displayed alone or with few additional flowers. The leaves are skillfully manipulated to camouflage the point where the flowers meet the container, furthering the illusion of the flower being real, which adds mystery and intrigue to this beautifully designed corner of a room. *Above:* If you have a basic collection of artificial flowers to choose from, it's easy to mix and match them in fresh new ways. Fruit branches, fiery red tulips, and blue forget-me-nots are the floral mainstays in this design. The white hyacinth flowers were the only special purchase made to add contrasting spiky shapes and neutral color balance to the design. Even the clear glass container has an impromptu look.

using fresh—or even dried—flowers. You do not have to worry that heat will open deliberately placed flower buds or that an air-conditioning or heating system will cause the arrangement to wilt and die. Aside from there being no messy preconditioning steps to follow, you also do not have to maintain an artificial arrangement. There is no dirty water to constantly change, and there are no dead flowers or foliage to constantly weed out. Nicer still is that artificial designs do not attract insects and also do not contain pollen, which can be a real problem for anyone with allergies.

Artificial designs can constantly be updated and can be disassembled in no time at all. Seasonal boundaries can be crossed with ease, because artificial flowers can be combined in all kinds of startling combinations. Use this freedom to create fantasy designs that would not be possible with fresh flower arrangements.

JOHN DEANE

Above: Traditional flowers—roses, lilies, and orchids—are used in a round, formal arrangement. Note, however, how casual flowers—chrysanthemums, alstroemeria, and forget-me-nots—also find a place in the design. Artificial flowers are excellent choices for designs such as this one that require strict adherence to shape to achieve their effect. *Right:* A large, open basket permits the arranger to mass a variety of artificial flowers without being concerned about how to get water to the flowers or breaking the stems, as is the case with fresh flowers. The focal pink peonies in this design are surrounded by light blue irises, burgundy and purple larkspur, purple bougainvillea, and yellow buttercups, which rhythmically intertwine throughout.

JOHN DEANE

Part of the freedom of working with artificial flowers is that once a design is created, it will last for as long as you wish. Seasonal combinations can quickly be created that will evoke a mood for months and can be recreated with minor variations the next year.

Now that the types of artificial flowers available are so numerous, it is possible to create a variety of arrangements for every season. In spring, informal arrangements of white, purple, yellow, and blue effectively evoke the season. Choose among the variety of blossoming artificial branches for this season, including dogwood, mountain laurel, quince, and apple blossoms. Tulips, anemones, daffodils, and irises also convey the mood of spring. Pastel-colored flowers matched with similarly colored baskets will also create a springlike air.

A potpourri of summery colors and flowers are also part of the charm of artificial flowers. Display an abundance of artificial flowers rich in texture and color throughout your home. Oversized combinations of snapdragons, roses, lilies, and other summer-blooming flowers can be created. This is the time of year to display the full range of your artificial flowers with glorious abandon. Colors, shapes, and textures should be casually mixed without fear of violating design rules.

Autumn arrangements can constantly be updated with the addition of live foliage. Chrysanthemums of all colors, marigolds, nasturtiums, and branches and grasses can all be displayed. Daisies, hyacinths, ranunculus, and other flowers from summer arrangements can be freely integrated with autumnal flowers. Choose rich, deep colors.

Winter designs can freely use flowers from all times of the year. When using artificial flowers, you are not limited by the lack of seasonal variety. For example, holly branches look stunning when matched with any number of artificial flowers. Such year-round favorites as camellias, roses, carnations, and daisies can be mixed with winter evergreen foliage for surprising results. Artificial flowers also look magnificent when integrated into Christmas trees and wreaths.

Artificial flowers allow the arranger to approach flowers from a new point of view. You are not limited by seasonal combinations, nor are you bound to use flowers in traditional containers. Instead, artificial flowers can be used in unexpected combinations and in completely surprising ways.

Artificial blossoms can evoke a seasonal feel as easily as fresh or dried flowers. The coloration of this design and the multiple textures of the materials indicate that fall is in the air. The use of thistle, bare branches, darkened foliage, and Spanish moss provides an effective fall-like backdrop for the vibrant flowers, which bring the design to life.

MAINTENANCE

Unlike fresh flowers and everlastings, artificial flowers allow the arranger a lot more leeway in handling them. High-quality artificial flowers are made up of a polyester blend that makes the flowers quite durable and relatively indestructible when compared to other arranging materials. Flower and leaf designs are printed directly on the flower fabric to create a very natural effect that also resists color changes.

To remove dust from artificial flowers, simply shake the flowers gently. Or if you wish to be more thorough, go over the flowers gently with a feather duster or with a blow dryer set on low-cool, blowing from the inner to the outer flower area.

If dust becomes lodged in an artificial flower, simply put the flower in a plastic bag with a little bit of salt. Allow the stem to protrude from the bag and gather the edges of the bag around the stem. Shake the bag lightly, and the dust should be completely dislodged.

Should an artificial flower somehow become stained, soak the petals of the flower—not the stem—in a small bowl of cold water with a capful of mild hand-washing detergent. Gently move the detergent around the petals until the stain is removed. Avoid getting the stem wet because artificial stems tend to unravel when moistened. Put the clean flower in clear water for a minute or two to rinse away residue from the detergent. Allow the flower to dry by drip-drying, by blotting it with paper towels, or by blow-drying it on a very low setting.

If there is any cotton content in the flower, treat it more delicately when you are washing it. Instead of using a blow-dryer or paper towels to dry it, just hang it up and let it air dry.

Another problem that you may encounter with artificial flowers is that sometimes they will lose their shape. To restore the natural-looking shape, set a flower or foliage on a soft towel and iron directly on each petal or leaf with the iron set on warm. Do not use the steam setting. With a few seconds of ironing, the flower's lifelike wrinkled and curved texture should begin to be restored.

An asymmetrical grouping of round flowers establishes an interesting rhythm in the design. The basket weave of the container is echoed in the wicker chest.

SCENTING

Just as the perfection of nature can be recreated with an artificial flower's appearance, the wonderful scent of flowers and herbs can be added to floral look-alikes. There are a number of oils that can be applied to flower arrangements with either an atomizer or an eyedropper. When an atomizer is used, measure out a solution of 4 parts oil to 1 part household alcohol, using the eyedropper as the measuring device. Be sure to add oils very sparingly to flowers, as too much can cause staining. With an atomizer, oils can be spritzed freely because the strength of the oils is diluted. Spritz the flowers in unobtrusive places such as on the underside of the flower and on the leaves. When an eyedropper alone is used, only the essence of the oil is applied. Therefore, cautiously apply a few drops at a time to the center of the flower. Pause between drops to determine if more scent is needed.

There are two basic types of oil to apply to arrangements for scent: essences of flowers and essences of fruit. When using flower oils, you can either exactly match the artificial flower with the oil or you can create startling contrasts and explore interesting combinations. Fruit essences are delightful additions to arrangements. A summer arrangement incorporating citrus leaves and either fresh or artificial citrus fruit would be given a very lifelike and delightful touch with the addition of lemon, lime, orange, or pineapple oils. Arrangements incorporating country garden flowers would truly seem to come to life with the addition of apple, strawberry, cherry, or raspberry scents. Such zesty oils are especially charming to use in the wintertime and during the holiday season, when they provide warm, soothing, ambient scents. Oil scents last for a week or more.

Such fragrant water scents as rose, lily of the valley, and orange blossom can also be applied to arrangements with wonderful results. They are applied to an arrangement with an atomizer and can be used freely because they are so diluted. These scents last for about a day at a time.

Cooking extracts of flowers, fruits, herbs, and spices can also be used to impart pleasing fragrances. You may need to dilute such extracts slightly. Extracts can be applied with either an eyedropper or an atomizer. They last for a very short period.

Another solution to scenting arrangements is the potpourri. They are excellent choices for use in and with flower designs because their main components are flowers, fruit rinds, spices, herbs, and sometimes oils. Potpourri combinations are as varied as are flowers. Simply select a mixture that especially pleases you and seems to impart life to the arrangement. Potpourri can either be arranged around the base of a design or can be displayed in an attractive box or bowl nearby the arrangement. You can alter the scent of a potpourri with the addition of your favorite oil.

Herbs and spices can also be used alone to scent a design. Simply sprinkle crushed herbs and spices over an arrangement or spread them at the base of the design. Cloves, basil, rosemary, coriander, dill, and any number of other substances —used individually or in combinations—lend an arrangement a very natural, charming scent that should last for a few days.

Oversized arrangements such as this one are particularly easy to carry out with artificial flowers. The choice of colors exemplifies rules of analogous combinations at play. Pastel pink is the dominant color, and it imparts a sense of lightness. Yellow and white play secondary roles, but provide focal spots of color. Red, a dark color, is used very sparingly to retain the airiness of the arrangement, while lending visual impact. Green foliage contributes to the analogous scheme, and nearby orange throw pillows provide a connecting link in the color spectrum.

CHAPTER SEVEN

STEP-BY-STEP ARRANGEMENTS

These nine step-by-step arrangements are designed to give you experience using a variety of media. They are good examples of how the many basic elements and principles of flower arranging come together when placing materials in a design, whether it is fresh, dried, or artificial.

Of course, these designs can be looked at as starting points for the imagination. You can substitute flowers and colors in a design or arrange the materials differently. The whole point of arranging is to develop the ability to respond to the particular situation at hand and to know when to emphasize particular design elements. Don't hesitate to endlessly vary these designs to suit your moods.

Step 1: This design exemplifies how a minimal arrangement in a simple, unornamented container is often one of the most effective designs you can create. Begin by arranging evoca-

BO PARKER

tively shaped branches in a clear-glass or crystal container. Because the arrangement itself is so stark, be sure to obtain a container with an interesting shape and simple beauty. Here, the container's unusual shape and lovely crystal texture contribute subtly to the design.

Distribute the branches throughout the container so that they reach out in a natural-looking configuration. The branches should be approximately twice the height of the total arrangement.

Step 2: Intersperse cream-colored calla lilies with the branches. Keep the elements of space and line and the principles of rhythm and unity in mind as you place them within the arrangement. Because calla lilies have a distinctive shape, no filler flowers are needed. Place the flowers at different heights and facing in different directions so that the arrangement has a unity to it without looking too calculated.

93

Step 1: For this arrangement, a glass container is used. Foam is used to anchor the flowers and is camouflaged with moss, which completely surrounds it. The arrangement builds on the basic framework established by the eight white roses that form a kind of triangle. The height of the arrangement itself, from the top of the container to the highest rose, is twice the height of the container. This design is somewhat traditional in that it incorporates traditional roses in a classic triangular shape. To make the arrangement not seem too rigid, however, the roses do not form a perfect triangle. Instead, they suggest the form of a triangle through their staggered heights.

Step 2: Echoing and building on the color scheme and form of the arrangement established by the roses, white freesias are incorporated. One airy-looking freesia extends beyond the reach of the tallest rose, giving the arrangement a light and flowing quality. Other freesias fill out the design framework created by the roses. Note that some of the buds are un-opened.

Step 3: Now that the predominant color scheme of white has been established, the middle color in the design—a blue-lavender imparted by the brodiaea—is added. Next, to add interesting spots of color in the design, pinkish- and garnet-colored scabiosa flowers are interspersed in the design. A balance of forms has been created with the harmonization of the roundness of the roses and the scabiosa blooms with the more elongated brodiaea and freesia forms.

Step 4: The design is completed with the addition of the filler flowers caspia and Queen Anne's lace, which fill out the design by helping to pull together the many components. The overall effect is airy, even though many individual elements are at play. The filler flowers ensure that no gaps are left in the design and help the eye make a smooth transition from one flower to the next.

BO PARKER

Step 1: The secret to the success of any design is establishing the correct foundation. For a large and seemingly complicated design such as this one, it is vital that the arranger spend extra time creating the framework. First, select a container that is large enough to hold a variety of heavy arranging materials. Here, a clear glass ginger jar is used. Add hydrangeas to the container. The ones used here are cream colored, with a tinge of pink on the petals that gives the fluffy blossoms a particularly enchanting effect. Arrange the hydrangeas so that their forms suggest a symmetrical triangle.

Next, add branches and foliage to build upon the design. The foliage should mirror the framework established by the hydrangeas. The branches should rise upward, with some foliage rising with them. Allow the expressive, natural curves of the foliage to be displayed to best advantage. The stems of the materials converging in the glass container do not need to be hidden. They have a very natural beauty that also serves a practical purpose: The converging of all the stems will form a natural holder for additional materials.

BO PARKER

Step 2: Add a number of tall, graceful lilies to the design. Their coloration should be a strong but not overpowering pink, speckled with bright spots, with color gently fading out around the edges. The pink of the lilies should pick up the pink on the petals of the hydrangeas.

The lilies, too, conform to the triangle already established by the framework materials; note that the heads of the flowers stay within the shape of the design. The lilies should not all be facing in the same direction. Let some turn naturally away. For an additional natural-looking touch and for the promise of future blossoms, include some unopened lily buds in the design. The lilies become the arrangement's focal flowers and also establish the dominant color in the design.

Step 3: Add several fragrant freesia to the design. Their bright hues provide stunning counterpoints to the lilies without competing with them for attention. As with the lilies, allow the freesia to face different directions so that the unforced, natural quality of the arrangement is enhanced.

Step 4: Finally, the yellow hues of the freesia are magnified and better appreciated when contrasted with the bright yellow centers of the gerbera daisies. Additionally, the introduction of white dendrobium orchids echoes the creamy color of the hydrangeas while picking up on the subtle white touches on the outer petals of the lilies and the frilled white petals of the daisies. Notice that the orchids vaguely suggest a triangular form in their placement, as do the daisies.

BO PARKER

Step 1: This arrangement proves once again that glass has a remarkable versatility and can be used in a number of ways in contemporary designs. Here, a circular glass bowl echoes the shape of the grape vines. These vines are looped in three individual rings and are held together unobtrusively with a bit of wire. Aside from being decorative, the grape vines also serve as a material for anchoring stems in place.

Step 2: Six stunning lilies, with rich green foliage attached, are now added to the design. Their two-toned coloration echoes the earthy hues of the grape vines. Four lilies are placed within the grape-vine rings, and two lilies are placed in the center. Notice that some unopened buds are included for future flowers that will extend the life of the arrangement. The placement of the lilies echoes and enhances the configuration of the grape-vine rings.

Step 3: The rich orange of the lilies is intensified by the addition of analogously colored montbretia blooms. Although lighter-colored flowers are generally chosen to extend beyond others in an arrangement, the brightly colored montbretia flowers are so small that they impart a very light look to the design. The proportional placement of the montbretia blooms lends the arrangement visual stability while echoing the upward thrust of the lilies and the grape-vine rings.

Step 4: Here one sees how analogous color schemes are truly effective in blending elements together while at the same time highlighting subtle color differences. Feathery-light yellow oncidium orchids extend beyond the limits of the arrangement on the sides, giving it a very airy appearance. The orchids are arranged in an asymmetrical fashion, which gives the arrangement a look of spontaneity. The sunny yellow tansies further play up this asymmetry and contribute bright highlights that bounce the eye from them to the yellow centers of the dominant lilies. Freesia hold it all together by providing a subtle accent.

TONY CENICOLA

TONY CENICOLA

Step 1: This dried design would be especially appropriate for autumn and the holiday seasons. Simply group dried and artificial elements against a neutral background of paper or fabric—or even on a mirror or tray—to create a charming display on a sideboard, mantelpiece, or table.

Begin by assembling the materials you will need. Pictured, clockwise, are three candles of different heights (the ones used in this design are red, but any color that complements a room's decor and harmonizes with the other elements of the design is appropriate), glycerine-treated and then gold spray-painted lemon leaves, multicolored strawflowers, papier-mâché fruit, glycerine-treated green lemon leaves tinged lightly with gold paint, and shiny bronze ribbon. The difference in the color of the leaves is not only a result of spray paint. The darker ones were left in glycerine longer than the lighter-colored foliage, so that the gold spray paint would take on a bronze cast.

Step 2: Arrange the candles in an asymmetrical triangle on the background surface. Add a grouping of leaves and fruit to the side of each candle as shown. Mix the green and bronze leaves if you wish.

Step 3: Add colorful strawflowers on top of each grouping of leaves in order to enhance the tones of the fruit and foliage.

Step 4: Arrange the ribbon around the outside edges of the ensemble, letting it meander gracefully among the various elements. Bring both ends of the ribbon around the front so that they meet in the center at the base of the candles. Light the candles for a festive effect.

TONY CENICOLA

Step 1: An ikebana-inspired design, this dried arrangement relies on very few materials to create its dramatic effect. A *kenzan* pincushion in the number 0 size provides sufficient support for this design because the materials are dried and do not need water.

Assemble the materials for the arrangement, pictured clockwise: a low, open bowl containing the *kenzan* pincushion; stripped bark pieces; three cattails, cut to three different heights of 21.5 inches, 20.5 inches, and 19.5 inches—your heights may differ as long as they are in similar proportion—three glycerine-treated flowering eucalyptus leaves that have been left in the preserving solution for three days, with their common stem strengthened by wire and floral tape; three strawflowers growing on a common stem; and green florist's tape, a wire cutter, and spool wire—the tools needed to work with the materials.

Step 2: Add the cattails to the pincushion so that they radiate in slightly different directions, as pictured. All materials will fit easily and snugly into the pinholder.

Step 3: Add the bark pieces so that they flank the cattails and gently echo their lines and suggest a fountain shape. The bark should extend about halfway up the cattails.

Step 4: The arrangement is complete when the eucalyptus leaves and strawflowers are added to the base of the design. Although the design is very spare, the effect is both striking and memorable.

JOHN DEANE

JOHN DEANE

Step 1: In this artificial arrangement, an unobtrusive, circular yellow container is complemented by the choice of linear flowers. Here, the flowers are approximately two-and-one-half times the size of the container itself, which is a very visually pleasing proportional relationship. Begin by inserting dramatic white larkspur into the container to loosely form a circular outline. The flowers should emanate in a fanlike manner from the container. Note how one larkspur stem actually cascades below the lip of the container.

Step 2: Deep green filler foliage is added around the base of the arrangement. One generous branch of greenery traces the path of the cascading piece of larkspur. The foliage aids in filling out the lower area of the arrangement.

Step 3: Continue adding foliage to the design. The foliage fills out the open areas left by the larkspur. There should be a dynamic interplay between the foliage and the larkspur, with the flowers appearing to boldly push through the greenery. Add pieces of lavender wisteria for a soft touch of realistic color. Position these flowers so that they follow the line of the larkspur that reaches down over the sides of the container, helping to almost completely obscure it. This way the emphasis is on the smooth rhythm of the arrangement and the eye is not distracted by the vase.

Step 1: Lilies are among the most popular flowers of all time, and there are many beautiful varieties of them that are reproduced as artificial flowers. Aside from their eye-catching shapes, lilies also come in a staggering array of colors and designs. For this arrangement, very lifelike rubrum lilies are used as the focal flowers. Obtain a circular container of a pink pastel shade that complements the tones of the rubrum lilies. After the lilies are placed in the foam base, use Spanish moss to camouflage the mechanics of the design; moss also lends the arrangement a realistic, natural look. Position the lilies in the design so that they curve in a gentle, natural-looking manner to add to the arrangement's fresh looking design, and use lilies that have buds attached to add to the effect.

Step 2: Add elegantly curved dracaena leaves to the design. They should bend gracefully away from the lilies so that they create an interesting shift of focus in the design. The effect of the two different materials curving in different ways infuses the arrangement with a feeling of movement.

Step 3: Lovely, crisp white lilies are then added to the arrangement. These flowers repeat the form of the lilies, but with their neutral coloration and smaller size, they magnify the beauty of the rubrums without competing with them. Place the white lilies at opposite sides of the design, with one grouping echoing the downward-reaching effect of the foliage and the other grouping providing an attractive contrast to the rubrums.

Step 4: Lovely white camellias, with buds attached, add another form to the design while magnifying the soft color scheme. These round flowers provide charming contrasts to the long leaves and also harmonize with the white of the lilies. The camellias also echo the global shape of the container.

106

JOHN DEANE

Step 1: Among the most prominent colors of nature are green and yellow, and this simple, completely unified arrangement of artificial flowers will create a very fresh mood in any room. A light green container is first filled with yellow dahlias that are of the same general tone as the green of the container. The dahlias should form a circle, with some flowers reaching higher in the center and others fanning out at staggered heights to form the curving sides of the circle. The dahlias should have dark green foliage attached. Allow some of the foliage to extend beyond the rim of the container. The addition of Spanish moss around the base camouflages the foam beneath.

Step 2: Add sprays of Queen Anne's lace to fill in the spaces between the flowers and foliage. The color of this filler flower warmly harmonizes with the creaminess of the dahlias. Position the Queen Anne's lace so that it follows the skeletal circular form established by the dahlias. However, since the Queen Anne's lace has a lighter color and an airier form than the dahlia, it can extend beyond the confines of the circle.

Step 3: To further anchor the base of the arrangement and continue the invigorating green-and-yellow color scheme, wandering Jew leaves are positioned to spill over the rim of the container. The leaves should extend in diverse directions along the bottom of the design, their striped forms intensifying the sense of movement.

Step 4: Spindle leaves, the final addition to this design, help define the outer boundaries while adding a variation to the color scheme. These leaves intensify the effects of the foliage in the design and provide smooth-textured contrast to the ruffles of the dahlias.

CHAPTER EIGHT

MIXING FRESH, DRIED, AND ARTIFICIAL FLOWERS

JOHN DEANE

One of the greatest pleasures of working with flower designs is having the freedom to bring together a variety of materials. This aspect of combining flower types adds a new level of complexity to arranging and requires careful forethought. Such designs are worth the extra effort because they break the visual monotony that can set in when too much of one kind of material is used.

In creating mixed designs of fresh, artificial, and dried flowers as well as adding in natural fruit and vegetable accessories, the arranger must be aware of the new varieties of texture, color, and form coming together. All these elements must be harmonized effectively. For example, the smooth perfection of artificial flowers must be matched with the natural idiosyncracies of fresh flowers so that differences between the two are not obvious. The special palette of colors of dried flowers requires careful matching with cut and artificial flowers.

KNOWING WHEN TO COMBINE TYPES
Whenever the vitality of a fresh arrangement seems to be waning because flowers and foliage are dying off, it is time to infuse the design with new life—in the form of artificial flowers. Using the basic stock of artificial flowers discussed in Chapter 6, it is possible to revitalize any fresh arrangement.

Conversely, because of their longevity, artificial flower designs often need variation to prevent them from becoming monotonous to the eye. If you have several artificial designs in your home, consider giving them a new look every week with the addition of fresh flowers. With the use of fresh flowers, one grouping of artificial flowers can have an infinite number of incarnations. Additionally, fresh foliage is a simple yet highly effective way of uplifting artificial designs. Because it is so easily obtainable in the wild, foliage is an inexpensive means of bringing visual freshness to a design.

Dried flowers are also natural accompaniments to designs incorporating either fresh or artificial blossoms. When a dried design needs perking up, the addition of artificial blossoms or foliage will immediately give it new life. Since both materials can be used indefinitely, the arrangement will not need any special care until you decide to change it again.

Striking forms of dried material are very effective when combined with fresh flowers. Thistles, pods, cattails, and branches combine easily with fresh flowers to create variegated looks that surprise the viewer.

Yet another dimension of flower arranging involves the use of fruits and vegetables. The use of natural accessories is a longstanding tradition of Flemish country arranging, which derives its inspiration from the still-life paintings of the Flemish School. In these arrangements, rich colors and varied forms are combined. Such fruits as oranges, apples, and grapes are artfully arranged around the base of the container. The Flemish School also influenced the popular nineteenth-century European custom of constructing two-tiered arrangements with the abundance of the garden strewn at the base of the design.

*Left: Garden-fresh tulips convey their vitality through their gracefully nodding forms. Lovely as they are, they need accompaniment to fill the space left by their bending over the container's side. **Above:** Soft-toned alstroemeria are an attractive choice for filling in the central area. Their stems are isolated from the water needed for the fresh tulips by floral foam set in a protective dish.*

JOHN DEANE

In creating arrangements that are meant to evoke the richness of a season or are created to accompany a meal, use of natural accessories is the perfect choice. Keep in mind that different vegetables and fruits have special characteristics that contribute to a design. Cabbage, eggplant, squash, and pineapple contribute interesting shapes and forms to a design. Smaller fruits and vegetables are best used in clusters to create cascading or transitional forms. Examples are grapes, radishes, red hot peppers, and brussels sprouts. Use such elongated forms as corn, carrots, and cucumbers to provide line in a design. And take advantage of the wide variety of rounded fruits and vegetables to provide circular contrast.

Among other natural accessories that can be freely used are stones of all kinds, sand, driftwood, shells, and anything that appeals to your imagination. Using a variety of materials artfully combined in new ways adds an exciting and daring dimension to flower arranging. Almost anything that originates in nature has a special visual appeal that can be taken advantage of in your designs.

ANCHORS FOR MIXED DESIGNS

There are some technical considerations to address when combining different types of flowers in a design. For the most part, you will want to avoid getting artificial flowers wet, although if you do choose to put them alongside fresh flowers in water, you can easily rewrap the stems after they disintegrate. Also, a floral foam can be used in such situations to provide water for the fresh flowers while anchoring the other materials. Except for some extremely resilient branches, you should not expose everlastings to water.

There are several solutions for isolating water in arrangements. One possibility is to position artificial and dried flowers so that they hang suspended in a container and do not touch

JOHN DEANE

Left: A subtle combination of pinkish-red, orange, yellow, and green artificial tulips, ranunculus, scabiosas, hyacinths, orchids, and foliage is complete in itself. Because of the longevity of artificial flowers, you may wish to update such an arrangement as the seasons change. Above: An attractive winter change of pace can be achieved by adding fresh star-of-Bethlehem and roses, as shown here. The flowers continue the analogous color scheme and enliven the arrangement with their rich fragrance.

the water below. Another solution is to use a small container of water within the larger container to hold the water for the fresh stems. The everlastings or artificial flowers can be positioned around this container and held in place by pebbles, marbles, or Styrofoam. Additionally, a cup-shaped pinholder capable of holding water can be used, or an ordinary pinholder can simply be set into a small container, such as a shallow glass dish, within a larger container. This way the water will be isolated from the artificial or dried elements. If holders are added to shallow bowls, they can be camouflaged with marbles, which will in turn hold the other flowers in place. Just remember to arrange the flowers and foliage carefully in the pinholder *before* water is added to prevent spillage. Use a turkey baster to add water to the arrangement.

COMBINATIONS THROUGH THE SEASONS

Throughout the year, you will have no doubt created a number of arrangements using different media. Some of the arrangements will be long-lasting artificial or everlastings designs that can be updated with different colors, while others will be transitory fresh designs that can be amplified with the addition of dried or artificial materials. Whatever the components of your arrangements, the element of color will be an important determinant in conveying the mood of the season.

Fresh flowers and foliage can be added to artificial designs as the seasons change. Artificial winter arrangements of white poinsettias and red camellias can be given a realistic look and scent with the addition of real evergreen foliage. This stunning color combination both signifies the holiday season and provides a dynamic complementary scheme. Real or artificial fruits associated with holidays—such as apples and oranges—can be added to designs for a festive air that provides vibrant color. Pearly white everlastings can be harmonized in such an arrangement along with mounds of artificial white camellias or chrysanthemums. The white flowers juxtaposed with the red and orange fruits and sprightly green foliage are very effective winter arrangements because they have a warm, welcoming look. Pots of artificial white amaryllis harmonized with fresh or artificial poinsettias in white or red are also quite effective.

Wreaths fashioned from birch twigs and decorated with artificial euphorbia branches, red orchid branches, and fresh variegated holly will warm a room with a burst of color. Everlastings wreaths, too, make charming holiday displays. Try combining preserved eucalyptus and heather with evergreens, white branches, and silver pods and cones. Pods can also be combined with fruits and nuts for a festive, bounteous effect. Lush wreaths combining a number of preserved flowers in monochromatic and analogous color schemes are also appropriate.

In wintertime, take advantage of the widespread availability of carnations, white pompons, chincherinchee (star-of-Bethlehem), and branches of quince, holly, and other greens. You can easily decorate Christmas trees with artificial or dried flowers, or you can attach small vials to the tree that can hold water, and wire the branches with green floral tape. Fresh or artificial fruit can also be wired to Christmas trees, either individually or in clusters. Add dried pods or seedheads spray-painted gold or silver to trees, or decorate trees entirely with sprays of dried limonium or gypsophila.

Below: The long-stemmed loveliness of these artificial poinsettias is accentuated by the slim crystal vase in which they are arranged. However, the arrangement has a somewhat naked air and needs more vitality. Right: Natural, inexpensive white daisies repeat the white-yellow color contrasts established by the poinsettias. Additionally, fresh pine fills out the lower areas of the design while punctuating the holiday spirit of the poinsettias. When adding fresh materials to vase arrangements, simply fill the lower part of the vase with water and allow the fresh stems to extend to that area while the artificial ones are held in place above the water by the mouth of the container.

JOHN DEANE

Above: An asymmetrical design of natural star-of-Bethlehem, carnations, and gladiolus is echoed by the charming twists taken by curly willow branches. The design, however, is clearly in need of additional flowers to fill out the base area and balance the strong upward thrust of the gladiolus. After you've gone through the trouble of picking out a variety of complementary blooms at the florist, you don't want to be caught without the final additional touches that fill out the design. It is at times like this when artificial flowers can come to the rescue. *Right:* The addition of alstroemeria, freesia, and scabiosas in harmonious colors gives this fresh arrangement a much-needed boost. When intermingled with natural flowers, artificial blooms seem all the more lifelike.

For such winter holidays as New Year's Day and Valentine's Day, there are many lively combinations of flowers that can be used. For the New Year, the traditional colors of white, red, silver, and green can be incorporated in a design that features winter-white artificial camellias or dahlias and real red-and-green holly branches in an ornate bowl. Special looks for Valentine's Day include real red roses juxtaposed with real or dried gypsophila that are accented by artificial red, pink, and white forget-me-nots and bleeding hearts. Since roses are so expensive, you may wish to use artificial roses in conjunction with inexpensive genuine carnations in pink or white.

Springtime provides a plethora of arranging possibilities because of the widespread availability of flowers and foliage. This is the time of year to let your imagination soar. Update your artificial winter foliage arrangements with the addition of either artificial or real wildflowers, tulips, lilies, or other spring flowers. This is where your basic stock of artificial flowers will come in handy, as most of the flowers are spring bloomers.

Less formal arrangements using the traditional spring colors of white, purple, yellow, blue, and pink are appropriate for this time of year. Because the theme of springtime is natural abundance, take advantage of your stock of dried and artificial flowers by freely displaying them all around your home alone or in combination with fresh flowers. Use plenty of pretty pastel-colored baskets as containers for your arrangements; massive displays of artificial lilies, tulips, daffodils, irises, crocuses, and other spring flowers can cascade dramatically out of unusual containers.

In summertime, the colors of nature become especially brilliant, and you can reflect this vibrancy in your arrangements. As in springtime, oversized baskets of artificial flowers of all kinds—snapdragons, peonies, lilies, roses, zinnias, and daisies—in every color of the rainbow are very appropriate. To show off the fresh beauty of garden-picked lilies and roses, amply display these flowers, but add artificial filler flowers to vary and extend the life of your designs.

Cool blue and pastel designs are very pleasing to the eye at this time of year. All-blue displays of artificial larkspur can be given a breath of life with the addition of fresh larkspur or a few fresh yellow freesia or white narcissus flowers. An arrangement of fresh pink roses can be amplified with the addition of artificial pink alstroemeria. Or an arrangement of artificial flowers in soft pastel shades can be given new drama when fresh flowers of the same kind but in deeper shades are added. The combinations of fresh and artificial flowers are truly endless. The trick is to enhance and vary whatever you have on hand—be it fresh or artificial—with the addition of a few flowers that completely renew and change the character of the arrangement through their colors and forms.

Autumn is the season when dried flowers are at their most effective, since they are generally associated with the harvest. Use a variety of interesting shapes such as repens star, monkeypods, sponge mushrooms, jinga pods, okra pods, and lotus pods to add fascinating shape and texture to arrangements. Color schemes can vary greatly. One traditional favorite is the earthy combination of cream, yellow, orange, and red expressed in arrangements using silica-dried zinnias, dahlias, pansies, and tulips harvested from the summer garden. Such an arrangement looks stunning when accented by glycerine-dried foliage and sprays of artemisia, goldenrod, and delphinium, which contribute graceful outlines to the design. Another possibility is to use an all-bleached color scheme. A variety of materials—including ferns, thistles, wild oats, wheat, and hydrangeas—can be combined in a dazzling and surprising white or off-white design. Such an arrangement could be enhanced with the addition of like-colored artificial flowers. Still another possibility for dried arrangements is to use a monochromatic color scheme of shades of brown. A brown woven basket with an interesting texture will set the tone for the arrangement, which can consist of dried dock, cattails, seed pods, pearly white everlastings, and artificial miniature daisies all in white, beige, and brown tones.

Additionally, many everlastings are available in a range of vivid colors made possible through dyeing. Rattail statice and gypsophila come in a range of attractive colors, which will

Rounded and elongated forms of natural and artificial materials are used to enhance this fresh design. The unlikely pairing of such common edibles as apples, oranges, peppers, and mushrooms with elegant lilies and other blooms will both delight and surprise the viewer. An arrangement such as this one makes a perfect centerpiece.

Above: A variety of dried materials—cattails, goldenrod, and grasses—charge this otherwise passive fresh design with energy through their upwardly surging forms. The dried materials are inserted above the water level in the vase. Additionally, artificial grapes are employed as natural accessories so a full spectrum of nature is represented. *Right:* Exotic in appearance and novel in its combinations of materials, this design creates a spiraling effect for the eye. The enormous protea in the center and surrounding pincushion protea demonstrate the many forms this interesting plant can take. A pink pineapple, orchids, and freesia provide fresh touches, while the purple allium and green club moss demonstrate how dried forms can add expressive qualities to natural designs. Artificial fruits at the base of the design complete the range of arranging materials used.

The mixture of fruits and flowers lends a whimsical, country-inspired air to this arrangement. Votive candles set in artichokes provide accent while the apples, pears, mushrooms, grapes, and lettuce suggest gustatory delights. To these fresh elements, dried branches are added to extend the design beyond its wicker container.

lend bright beauty to both artificial and fresh designs. Everlastings and artificial flowers are wonderful flowers to pair in autumn, as many striking textural and color combinations can be created. For example, dried zinnias in rust tones combine beautifully with artificial orange and burgundy ranunculus. Dried and colored sprays of orange wheat can also be added to this analogously colored arrangement. Artificial ranunculus in deep purple tones combines nicely with similarly colored dried liatris and thistle. Beautiful bare branches and preserved foliage can act as finishing touches to this combination design.

Also use live, brilliantly colored foliage from the garden in your autumn arrangements. Fresh azalea and forsythia foliage mix gloriously with artificial flowers or dried grasses. Or use fresh golden and orange marigolds harvested from the fall garden and mix them with artificial flowers that shimmer in the same tones: chrysanthemums, nasturtiums, helichrysums, and dahlias.

Other strong elements in autumn arrangements are fruits and vegetables. Designs incorporating these natural accessories are particularly appropriate in dining-room settings and will completely embody the mood of Thanksgiving. Use dried gourds, Indian corn, and mushrooms alongside pumpkins, nuts, and real and artificial apples, grapes, and pears. Preserved berry branches, such as buckthorn sprayed with varnish, are also attractive both used alone and incorporated in arrangements with fresh or artificial flowers.

As the seasons change, so does the palette of colors and range of materials that are associated with each. By recognizing these seasonal differences, it is possible for the arranger to both evoke the season through a design or present an element of surprise by suggesting a hint of the season to come, such as an autumn design that incorporates light shades of spring or a winter design that juxtaposes traditional poinsettias with summer daisies.

Never before has the arranger had so many choices for designing with flowers. Fresh flowers are now widely available at all times of the year; new techniques for drying and dyeing flowers have introduced more lifelike color and variety in this medium; and artificial flowers have reached new heights of realistic beauty. By taking advantage of these breakthroughs, flower arrangers can endlessly experiment with new styles and discover surprising new floral combinations.

SOURCES

FRESH FLOWERS

BALL SEED CO.
P.O. Box 335
West Chicago, IL 60185

BLUESTONE PERENNIALS INC.
7211 Middle Ridge Rd.
Madison, OH 44057

BUSSE GARDENS
635 E. Seventh St.
Rt. 2, Box 13
Cokato, MN 55321

CARROLL GARDENS
444 E. Main St.
Box 310
Westminster, MD 21157

DELAWARE VALLEY WHOLESALE
FLORIST
4800 Dahlia St.
P.O. Box 1138
Denver, CO 80201

INTERNATIONAL GROWERS
EXCHANGE
17142 Lahser Rd.
Detroit, MI 48219

KENNICOTT BROTHERS CO.
2660 N. Clybourn Ave.
Chicago, IL 60614

POWELL'S GARDENS
Rt. 2, Box 86
Princeton, NC 27569

ANDRE VIETTE FARM & NURSERY
Rt. 1, Box 16
Fishersville, VA 22939

WHITE FLOWER FARM
Litchfield, CT 06759

EVERLASTINGS

KNUD NIELSEN CO.
P.O. Box 746
Evergreen, AL 36401

VANS, INC.
3730 W. 131st St.
Alsip, IL 60658

ARTIFICIAL FLOWERS

ALDIK ARTIFICIAL FLOWER CO.
7651 Sepulveda Blvd.
Van Nuys, CA 91405

CAFFCO
P.O. Box 3508
Montgomery, AL 36193

DESIGNER ACCENTS
10614 King William Dr.
Dallas, TX 75220

UN JARDIN . . . EN PLUS
24 W. 57th St.
New York, NY 10019

CONTAINERS

MILTON ADLER
501 Madison Ave.
Atlantic City, NJ 08401

BLENKO GLASS CO.
P.O. Box 67
Milton, WV 22541

FRANKLIN CHINA
112 Terwood Rd.
Willow Grove, PA 19090

HOOSIER GLASS
P.O. Box 756
Kokomo, IN 46901

VINCENT LIPPE
11 E. 26th St.
New York, NY 10010

MOTTAHEDEH
225 Fifth Ave.
New York, NY 10010

TOSCANY IMPORTS
245 Fifth Ave.
New York, NY 10016

INDEX

E

F

G

H

I

L

M

N

O